A GARDENER'S GUIDE TO

Cottage
gardening

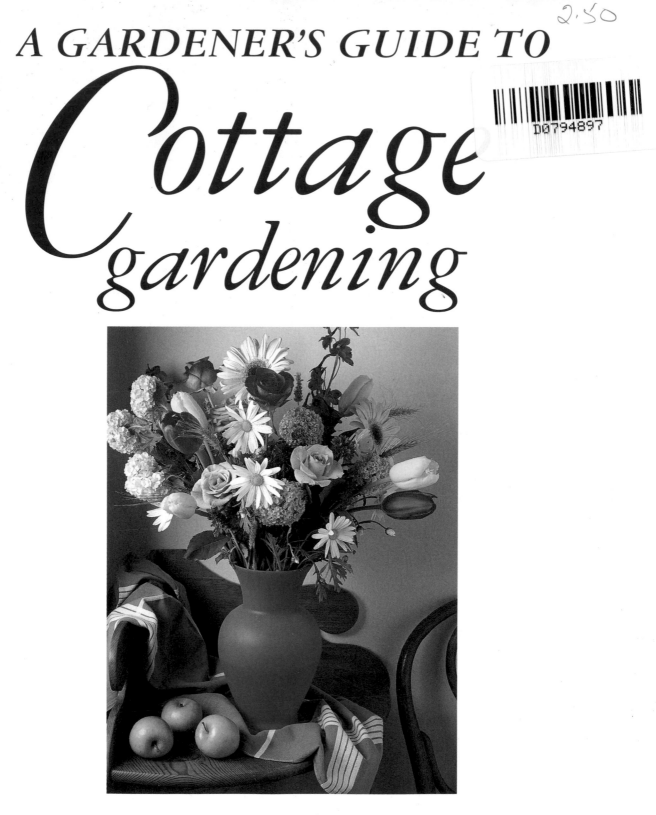

Editor Valerie Duncan
Series Editor Graham Strong

MEREHURST

Merehurst Ltd, Ferry House, 51-57 Lacy Road, Putney, London SW15 1PR

CONTENTS

CREATING A COTTAGE GARDEN

ABOVE LEFT: A romantic colour scheme in blue, lilac, pink and white is here carried out with long-blooming summer flowers: pink petunias, blue salvias, *Gaura lindheimeri* and roses, against a backdrop of a fine blue spruce. ABOVE CENTRE: A path through a shaded corner is dressed up for spring in white honesty and sweet bluebells, with a flowering branch of white *Viburnum plicatum* in the foreground. ABOVE RIGHT: Old-fashioned picket fences suit just about any style of house, from the humblest to the grandest. The flowers grown here are deep pink penstemons, cosmos and white roses. OPPOSITE: This richly-planted border in front of a traditional thatched cottage is packed with a variety of popular cottage garden plants, including lupins, iris and geraniums. INSET: Yellow Californian poppies and blue iris.

Fashions change in horticulture as they do in all aspects of life. A few years ago, the cry was 'Easy maintenance!', the idea being that we were all so busy doing the exciting things that the twentieth century made possible (watching television, travelling, driving fast cars, eating in gourmet restaurants and working long hours to pay for it all) that we had no time for such old-fashioned chores as working in the garden.

But then some people realised that gardening can still be fun, and that while an easy-maintenance garden of trees, paving and ground-cover plants can indeed be very beautiful, there is great satisfaction to be gained in watching the growth of things that we have actively cultivated.

And so cottage gardens came back into fashion, and it looks as though they will be with us for a very long time to come. For this is the style of gardening that offers most scope to the enthusiastic gardener, and you can make a beautiful cottage garden on a tiny plot just as well as you can on a big one.

But just what is a cottage garden? For that matter, what is a cottage? Originally, a cottage was the dwelling of a farmer or someone who worked on the estate of one of the great landowners, and if cottage gardens had a distinctive style it grew from the way of life of their inhabitants. These were people with little money and less leisure to spend on ornamental gardens.

The plants that the cottagers of old grew on these little plots of land were mainly vegetables and fruit trees, and the herbs that could be used for home-made medicines. They were grown from cuttings and seeds that they exchanged with neighbours and friends. It may seem surprising to us today just how many of our favourite garden plants were originally grown for their usefulness rather than their beauty. Roses, lilies, hollyhocks, foxgloves, calendulas, lily-of-the-valley and forget-me-nots, were all commonly grown plants which combined beauty with usefulness. (We might wonder

ABOVE LEFT: Bright red poppies sit in front of a generous assortment of perennials, giving the air of lush and informal planting that is characteristic of the cottage garden style.

ABOVE RIGHT: Nowadays we have more time to enjoy our gardens than the cottagers of old. So, whatever its size, make room in your garden for a table and chairs where you can entertain your guests, or simply relax and enjoy the results of your handiwork.

whether sometimes the usefulness was an excuse for the beauty. How often do we justify some small luxury on the grounds that it might be useful?)

There was no room in these early cottage gardens to segregate the plants by type the way we do now – fruit trees here, flowers there, vegetables somewhere else – and so they were all grown together. This happy blending of plants of all types is the legacy of the cottagers to modern gardens.

Not that these gardens were untidy hodgepodges: it was a matter of pride to have a neat and attractive front garden. (The back gardens tended to be filled with washing lines, sheds and chicken runs.) The plants were arranged to give pleasure to the eye – tall hollyhocks at the back, beds edged in lavender or pinks to create a neat finish, and roses trained around doors and along fences.

MODERN COTTAGE GARDENS

Times have changed and we are now wealthy and leisured to a degree that the old cottagers could only dream of. We are no longer dependent on the produce of our gardens for our dinner, and we can indulge in creating gardens for no other reason than simply for our pleasure.

Yet most of us live in smallish houses and our gardens are getting smaller all the time: not for us the splendours of massed trees and banks of shrubs or great sweeps of immaculate lawns and formal rose gardens with twenty bushes of the same variety to a bed. Like the early cottagers, our scope is limited, and like them we find our pleasure in gardening on a small scale – the small view, focusing on the scent of a rose or the graceful

ABOVE: The cottage gardens of old were very much working gardens, where the cottagers would grow their vegetables and fruit. In this garden the owner has followed in the old tradition by creating a cottage garden potager.

TOP: The gravel path that winds through this cottage garden can scarcely be seen for the profusion of flowers and foliage that tumble over the edges or that have self-seeded amongst the stones and gravel.

LEFT: Their ease of cultivation and wide range of flowers and foliage make the hardy geraniums invaluable plants for the modern cottage garden border.

lines of a lily – not massed by their hundreds but in three of this and four of that. Whenever we grow many different flowers in a relatively small space, we are indeed gardening in the cottage style.

Some gardeners feel very strongly that a modern cottage garden should be a re-creation of an old one. They choose to limit what they grow in their cottage garden to 'old-fashioned' flowers, and they worry about whether it is 'authentic' to have a lawn or to grow flowering shrubs.

If you live in an old cottage (or indeed in a grand old house) you might care to take this approach, it is in a sense the horticultural equivalent of restoring and furnishing a house 'in period'. But while it can be fun to re-create an 'authentic' cottage garden there is no need to keep to such a strictly limited style if you do not feel that you want to. The cottage garden style is a manner of gardening that is as flattering to a modern house as it is to an old one.

Let your approach and your layout be simple and straightforward, and designed to suit your own personal requirements and interests, and those of your family. If you need a lawn for the children to play on, or a terrace or patio on which to sit and talk to friends, or entertain them to a meal, then make them. Adapt the style to suit you.

Plant trees and shrubs for shade and privacy; and indulge yourself in your favourite plants and flowers, whether they are old or new, mixing and matching them with each other and with herbs and edible plants. Some of the plants you choose may be modern hybrids, some may be plants that the cottagers could never afford, but many will be the old-fashioned, easy to grow favourites. For, as the saying goes, fashions may change, but beauty, never!

ABOVE LEFT: Hollyhocks are among the first plants you turn to when planting your cottage borders. Here they are planted with shrubby lavateras against a warm brick wall in front of trained fruit trees.

ABOVE RIGHT: If allowed, perfumed climbers and wall shrubs soften house walls and frame windows. That way, they'll mingle seductively with the scent from windowboxes like this one planted with stocks.

PLANNING AND PLANTING

The cottage garden embodies an idyll of rural life set against a background of bulging thatch, lichen-encrusted stone and leaded lights. There's no doubt that it has a romantic, beguiling quality that holds many of us in its spell and it has become a style that is universally admired. Part of the charm is that it looks so effortlessly achieved, as though it hasn't actually been planned at all, but has just grown up out of the surrounding landscape. It would be misleading, though, to suggest that maintaining a cottage garden is as leisurely as the once yearly clip over with the shears that a heather garden requires. Like many things in life, it reflects the effort and imagination we put in. But exactly how is it done? Here are some ground rules for ingredients, that, when assembled, should fulfil all your most romantic yearnings, in a cottage garden at least!

HALLMARKS OF THE COTTAGE GARDEN
- A framework of paths and walls built using local materials – stone, brick, cobbles and gravel – will echo the construction of the house.
- An element of self-seeding is essential. Plants popping up out of cracks and crevices in walls and paving will look more spontaneous than any attempt at introducing them.
- Naturalise bulbs in rough cut grass, like snowdrops, crocus, narcissus and snakeshead fritillary. They look charming amongst wizened apple trees in flower, with speedwell running through the grass, reflecting the blue sky above.
- Encourage native species to encroach on the boundaries. Plants from hedgerows and woodland, such as nettle-leaved bellflower, red campion, bluebells and anemones, can be

encouraged and will blur the division between country and garden. Don't raid the countryside for them, though!

• The scene is incomplete without a generous assortment of plants, including cottage perennials, climbers, shrubs, herbs, alpines, annuals and bulbs, to give a rich profusion of flowers, foliage and perfume to clothe walls, fill borders and cheer up containers. Choose old-fashioned varieties if possible, not highly bred, often over-sized versions, that have lost the natural character of the species.

Sometimes it's easier to decide what to include in your layout by identifying 'no go' areas. Here are a list of ingredients that definitely won't fit into the traditional cottage garden.

OUT OF CONTEXT

The following plants and features will strike a discordant note:

- Dwarf conifers – pass these over in favour of clipped box, holly and yew.
- Rock gardens – plant dry stone walls and raised beds with alpines instead.
- Deep lawn edges with soil thrown back in a steep camber.
- Bamboos, hybrid tea roses, beds planted exclusively with heathers.
- Modern paving materials, classical statues and urns, balustrading.

LEARNING FROM THE PAST

If you've got your sights set on recreating a traditional cottage garden layout, it is worth looking again, briefly, at the significance attached to the gardens and specific plants they contained. During the latter part of the nineteenth century a farm labourer would have

ABOVE LEFT: Each of these three plants will perpetuate itself freely from seed. Orange Pilosella has worked its way up through our native Tutsan (*Hypericum androsaemum*). Lady's mantle provides the edging.

ABOVE RIGHT: *Smyrnium perfoliatum* is an eye-catching biennial that resembles a euphorbia, but is in fact related to cow parsley. It blends in beautifully with purple honesty rising above a haze of forget-me-nots.

ABOVE: With a rich scent of myrrh, the shrub rose 'Constance Spry' is of recent origin but has the character of old-fashioned roses and looks lovely with honeysuckle growing nearby.

TOP: Lavender and cottage pinks make ideal companions for roses. Here David Austin's recent introduction 'Scepter'd Isle' is further enhanced by the deep red *Astrantia* 'Hadspen Blood'.

ABOVE RIGHT: For hot, dry beds on the fringes of the garden, imposing Scotch thistle will soon form self-perpetuating colonies as it has among these opium poppies. The idea would also work well in gravel.

earned as little as eight shillings (40 pence) for a week's work on the land, so his garden provided plenty of food, a point graphically illustrated in *Larkrise to Candleford* by Flora Thompson: 'The men took great pride in their gardens... Fat green peas, broad beans as big as a halfpenny, cauliflowers a child could make an armchair of, runner beans and cabbage and kale, all in their season... A few slices of bread and home-made lard flavoured with rosemary, and plenty of green food "went down good" as they used to say.'

Nowadays, ornamental plants will certainly dominate the modern cottage garden, but if you want fruit and vegetables tucked in among the blooms in your garden, try gooseberries, rhubarb, red cabbage, lettuce and curly kale – all will appeal to the eye and the tastebuds.

It is great fun to entertain your guests with a few amusing anecdotes. Include the following plants in your garden scheme and you'll have the perfect excuse to introduce a good story.

• Cottagers would take comfort in the knowledge that their tight cluster of houseleeks (*Sempervivum*) growing on the roof tiles would protect their property from being struck by lightning.

• As well as providing food for birds and looking informal enough to be planted in the cottage garden, a rowan tree was said to ward off witches.

• Colourful plants were given colourful names by country folk. Once you have heard the red valerian (*Centranthus ruber*) referred to as 'Welcome home husband though never so drunk', you'll never see it in quite the same light again. It does have a habit of wandering around the garden in a rather aimless fashion!

ABOVE: Avoid the regimented parks department approach to tulips by planting them in clumps so they emerge through carpets of poached-egg flower and dainty violas.

TOP: In wilder areas of the cottage garden why not let vigorous carpeters like snow in summer and suckering spurge cypress loose among self-seeding blue alkanet, aquilegia and pot marigold.

ABOVE LEFT: To encourage a rich variety of wild flowers to grow like these you must start with a poor soil and fine grass seed mixture. A corner summerhouse made in a vernacular style makes a fine viewpoint.

ADAPTING THE STYLE

If you're lucky enough to live in a honey-coloured Cotswold stone cottage then you have the perfect excuse to adopt the cottage garden look, hook line and sinker, and are probably already collecting the free range eggs and filling your hanky drawers with lavender bags. But what if you live in a relatively new house or in a town or city semi or in a row of Victorian terraces? Don't worry, because the look travels well. It's only likely to jar against the backdrop of an ultra modern steel and glass style house or a formal Georgian town house with a central door and windows arranged symmetrically either side. Elsewhere you can enjoy the rich variety of planting or those rustic eye-catchers like staddle stones, thatched bird houses and old mangles. Cottage garden practices bring with them many advantages. A mixed country style hedge, for example, is likely to attract a rich variety of birds into your garden, more even perhaps than in a country setting, especially if surrounded by prairie style, intensively managed farmland. It is certainly a more attractive proposition than a sombre wall of leylandii conifers or surrounding your plot with stark off-the-peg mass-produced fence panels. With hazel, hawthorn, holly, guelder rose and beech in your hedge and carpets of daffodils, bluebells and wood anemones beneath, it is not hard to imagine yourself in the very heart of the countryside.

The more we begin to think about the practical requirements our garden has to fulfil, the less realistic it becomes to live inside a chocolate box cover. Families in particular put stresses and strains on our plots, and play areas and cycle tracks for the children, parking spaces for cars and caravans and utility areas for drying clothes and storing dustbins must all be considered at the outset. Privacy and screening are also a primary concern in gardens

ABOVE: This lovers' knot has been planted with low interlocking hedges of lonicera and santolina and filled in with pansies and forget-me-nots. Wallflowers tie the garden neatly together like a yellow ribbon right outside a cottage window. The centrepiece is tulips planted in an upturned rhubarb forcing pot. Because the hedges are both evergreen they will give a permanent structure that can be bedded out around and in between them twice a year. Nasturtium 'Alaska Mxd' and pot marigold 'Fiesta Gitana Mxd' would make a pleasing summer scheme.

that are surrounded by houses, and strategically placed evergreens are likely to be essential. Don't worry. By breaking up the garden into a series of smaller units, it's quite possible to zone all your wants and needs so they don't conflict one with the other.

PATIOS, PATHS AND BOUNDARIES

The patio is probably the most fundamental feature in the garden nowadays and even the most hardworking 'cottagers' will welcome the opportunity to sit back and relax with a drink and a biscuit and gaze out on their handiwork. Large wall-to-wall strips of buff paving slabs pointed with mortar across the back of the house are most unlikely to achieve the desired look for they will deny plants the chance to seed themselves and the garden to appear to flow right up to the house walls. Here are some tips to enable you to integrate your patio into the cottage style:

- A paved area that combines together three or four surfaces in a rich pattern adds contrast of colour and texture.
- Include pockets of loose-laid materials like pebbles, gravel and setts that can be put down on sand (or even soil if it is light and free draining). You can then plant herbs and alpines to grow through them, sow seed of hardy annuals or let nature take its course and see what seeds itself.
- Rather than have one huge patio, consider building two or three smaller ones facing different points of the compass, or follow the sun around your garden and build, for example, a west-facing patio to catch the evening sun.
- Decorate your patio with clusters of pots, stone troughs and an old watering

can or two. Go mad and lay old timber beams, fire-baskets, fossils, millstones and even bottles (neck down) into your paved mosaic for a slightly eccentric look.

• Let the planting wrap itself around your patio in a soft embrace. You'll enjoy the proximity of scented leaves and blooms and your patio will quickly achieve a look of maturity beyond its years.

With your patio in place, the next logical step is to link it to the rest of the garden through a network of paths. Traditional cottage garden layouts were surprisingly formal with a straight path up the plot (often to the front or back door) bisected by other paths coming off at right angles. The reason they don't appear so formal is that once plants have spilled over and seeded into the paths, the hard lines are softened and disguised. These grid systems of paths will result in the most authentic layouts and if each path leads to, say, a seat in a perfumed bower, a sundial or, more practically, the tool shed or hen house, the garden will be both rewarding and easy to work in. You may like to set as an objective being able to reach all your borders from a pathway (even if it's with a hoe) to keep the soil off your boots as much as possible.

As with patios, combining materials in your paths will make them a feature in themselves.

CHOOSING MATERIALS.
Choose from old materials:
• Broken and random rectangular York stone.
• Salvaged bricks, stable pavers and granite setts.

ABOVE LEFT: Don't be reluctant to sow varieties of annuals that are more highly bred than their wild counterparts when they're as big an improvement as these 'Fiesta Gitana' strain of pot marigolds. They are a lovely contrast to *Fuchsia* 'Mrs Popple'.

ABOVE RIGHT: Red cabbage is handsome enough to mix with flowers from early summer right through to the autumn. 'Ruby Ball' acts as a foil to pansies and Sweet Williams.

RIGHT: This cast iron harrow has been used to support a handsome collection of striped marrows as their skins ripen and harden in the late summer sunshine. The cosmos, behind, seed in this garden from year to year.

ABOVE: Old clay roof tiles laid sideways on don't need to be arranged as expertly as these, though they do undeniably make a beautifully mitred corner.

ABOVE: These square concrete block pavers have been tumbled in a giant mixer to age them. Creeping thyme and chamomile provide further softening.

ABOVE: Old timber beams are used to box in salvaged bricks and make a patio that is almost a mirror image of the cottage walls.

- Quarry tiles, clay roof tiles laid on edge.
- Roof slates broken up into small pieces.

New materials:

- Paving slabs that have been cast from moulds taken from older materials such as Victorian flagstones.
- Bricks and concrete pavers that have been 'tumbled' to knock off the corners and give an aged finish.
- 'Antique' look concrete bricks and tiles that have been made to look like clay and terracotta.
- Pebbles, gravel and chippings.
- Stock and brindles with several soft colours in their make up rather than raw red engineering bricks.

BOUNDARIES

As well as the country-style hedge mentioned earlier, fences made from natural materials, although more expensive than more widely available alternatives, lend an instant flavour of the countryside and an almost medieval character. Peeled, woven willow and hazel hurdles and tree heather panels look superb even without clothing plants. Low lengths of willow can be used to define the edge of beds and miniature split hazel 'gates' are a delight along cottage borders or even as a support for a top-heavy plant.

Yew, quickthorn, beech, box and field maple are all good choices for hedges; Leyland cypress is definitely not.

PLANTING UP YOUR GARDEN

There's no denying that we are spoilt for choice when it comes to choosing plants for our garden nowadays and cottage gardeners of old would have taken great delight in the many new and improved varieties of old favourites and even some plants that would be unknown to them. However, if a traditional style of planting is your aim, then there are species that just don't sit comfortably with all those hollyhocks, rambling roses and Canterbury bells. Plants of exotic or contemporary appearance like phormiums and cordylines, for example. Similarly, aristocrats like tree magnolias and large-leaved rhododendrons would have represented a king's ransom to a cottage gardener. Here is a list of classic varieties that are guaranteed to exist in harmony. You will find out about many of them later in the book.

CLASSIC COTTAGE GARDEN PLANTS

Herbaceous perennials – hollyhocks, pinks, lady's mantle (alchemilla), lupins, delphiniums, Hattie's pincushion (astrantia), bleeding heart (dicentra), Michaelmas daisies, auriculas, pyrethrums, poppies, irises, bellflowers, cowslips and primroses.
Shrubs – lavender, rosemary, flowering quince, old roses, daphne, hardy fuchsia, mock orange, buddleja, lilacs.
Annuals and biennials – wallflowers, Sweet Williams, double daisies, pansies and violas, cornflowers, love-in-a-mist, nasturtiums, candytuft, Canterbury bells, larkspur, stocks, sunflowers.
Herbs – many would have been grown for their medicinal properties: feverfew, fennel, comfrey, lemon balm, chamomile, chives, sage, thyme, rue, hyssop, marjoram, mint.

ABOVE: Who could imagine a more charming spring scene than this thriving colony of red crown imperials marching through daffodils and past stone walls encrusted with aubrieta right up to the cottage door. Of course, a garden that is too reliant on spring bulbs will lack interest later in the year, so aim to have plenty of perennials planted in between to keep up the momentum.

ABOVE LEFT: Everything except the kitchen sink is a bit of an exaggeration, but by mixing different types of paving units and even including this iron firebasket you can create an interesting patterned mosaic.

ABOVE RIGHT: Although dry stacked bricks laid like this may at first appear unstable, surprisingly, they will in fact make a sturdy wall that requires little expertise to build and has a pleasing, informal quality that makes a perfect backdrop for informal cottage garden planting.

Self-seeding plants — honesty, forget-me-not, Welsh poppy, red valerian, verbascum, fennel, columbine, foxgloves, nettle-leaved bellflower, love-in-a-mist, opium poppy, Scotch thistle. *Bulbs* — crown imperials, Madonna and martagon lilies, snowdrops, narcissus, aconites and anemones.

CHOOSING YOUR PLANTS

Most cottage garden plants are by their very nature obliging and easy to please, but it is still important to consider your own unique conditions before rushing out and buying on impulse. Choose plants that will tolerate or even thrive in hot sun or dry shade, wet sticky soil or soil that is alkaline (limey). Exposure too is a factor. Tall delphiniums would soon be blown over in windy sites and in a low-lying spot you may find that frost collects and plants may be damaged (fruit blossom, for example) whereas further up the slope the blooms are untouched.

YEAR ROUND COLOUR

As you'll see from the list of recommended plants, cottage gardens are a jostling mixture of everything from a tree to a bulb or hardy annual, but in our desire to recreate those idyllic cottage cameos typified by the watercolours of Helen Allingham it's easy to plant for summer at the expense of wintertime and those cottage borders must have reverted to a forest of sticks by November. Evergreens are needed to give backbone so aim for at least a quarter of your plants to retain their leaves by choosing the likes of box, holly,

viburnum, yew, elaeagnus, spotted laurel and mahonia; berries and bark will also add much appeal.

We don't often consider the fact that a double red peony is only at its best for a few days, but it's important to weigh up a plant's flowering period, particularly if space is limited. Compare this with *Aster* x *frikartii* or *Coreopsis verticillata* that give months of bloom. Some plants have such charisma that you accept their shortcomings; rust disease on hollyhocks, for example.

WORKING TO A BUDGET

If you're on a tight budget, here are some ideas to save money:
- Grow perennials from seed. Most seed catalogues list varieties that can be readily grown from seed. Some like achillea, coreopsis and *Lobelia cardinalis* will produce a few flowers in the first year.
- Look out for big clumps of perennials for sale in small pots. These can be split in spring and early summer into two or even three separate pieces.
- Swap plants with friends and neighbours, but identify any incomers first in case they take over the garden!

SPACING

A good rule of thumb when planting out perennials is to put in five plants per square metre but such large blocks of a single variety may not be in keeping with the spontaneous explosion of colour where plants jostle and compete for space and attention. Neither will a

ABOVE RIGHT: A weathered statue of Pan sits alongside a fallen apple tree bough in this stark wintry scene. As he is a woodland creature, the chosen setting for Pan is perfect.

ABOVE LEFT: Staddle stones were used to raise wooden grain stores off the ground and secure them against rats and would inevitably find their way into cottagers' plots. This lichen-encrusted top contrasts beautifully with a carpet of aubrieta.

ABOVE LEFT: Clematis and honeysuckle are beginning to entwine in a delightful duet along an old wall where the niches have been filled with a pensioned-off teapot, houseleeks and a terracotta finial.

ABOVE RIGHT: It's hard to imagine a more apt and romantic viewpoint than this from which to look out on your garden. This willow seat has already begun to take on an air of permanence with ivy clambering up the sides and poking through the weave.

border carefully regulated for height from front to back give the desired effect. The best technique is to build a framework of permanent plants to start with by laying out key trees and evergreen and deciduous shrubs first, using their heights and spreads after ten years to guide you. Then fill in the gaps with cottage perennials and annuals. Include self-seeders and they will soon get a foothold, and in the autumn underplant with bulbs. Do any fine tuning in the second year for most plants won't object to being moved about. You may wish to avoid potential colour clashes, orange with pink for example, or not be too precious about colour themes and concepts. Contrast, however, is important so juxtapose tall spires with round shapes and low spreaders every now and then for a stimulating picture.

GROUND PREPARATION AND PLANTING

Here are some useful tips:
- Keep off the soil when wet and avoid planting when the ground is frozen or waterlogged.
- Dig in plenty of organic matter: garden compost, spent mushroom compost or composted bark for example.
- Stand bare-root or container-grown plants in water for an hour before planting so they are thoroughly soaked.
- Prepare a planting hole deep and wide enough to allow the roots to spread.
- A mulch of bark chippings or cocoa shell around your plants will keep in moisture and suppress weeds.
- Keep plants well watered and staked (if necessary) and watch for pests and diseases.

EYE-CATCHERS

Perhaps even more enjoyable than getting your plants into position is adding those finishing touches that catch the eye and add that little spark of magic that singles out an average garden from something really special. It's very much like positioning your favourite ornaments in a room that's just been decorated. It also requires a similar level of thought, for just plonking down your cottage props wherever there's a gap will rarely succeed. Often it's fun to come across an ornament by chance, tucked away perhaps amongst planting. A garden roller in the orchard half concealed by flowers and grasses is more romantic than one stranded on the patio. Even staddle stones look more permanent when 'anchored' by carpeting plants at their base.

Here are a selection of suitable props for an authentic working cottage garden environment:
- Eye-catchers – these should be unpretentious, ideally the sort of everyday objects that would be in the garden anyway: boot scraper, besom (twig broom), wooden wheelbarrow, old watering can, garden roller, bee hive, stone water trough, seakale and rhubarb forcers, hens, well-head (beware of twee versions), pig sty, outdoor privy, sundial, cast-iron pump.
- Planters – half oak barrels, simple hand-thrown earthenware pots, stone troughs, galvanised baths and dolly tubs.

When everything's in place, sit back in your woven armchair and admire your handiwork, but don't let the grass grow under your feet!

ABOVE: Cats are guaranteed to find the warmest, cosiest spot and no cottage garden is really complete without one. They have a way of watching you at work as if to say, 'I wouldn't do it like that'.

TOP: The best place for rhubarb forcing jars is in the rhubarb patch and likewise seakale forcing jars. Seakale is a handsome vegetable with clouds of white flowers and leathery grey leaves.

ABOVE LEFT: Cast iron garden rollers have long ceased to be an essential piece of gardening equipment, but they still make an impression, abandoned, like this one, in an overgrown patch.

$\mathscr{A}$NNUALS *are bursting with life and energy. Most live for only six months or so, but it's definitely life in the fast lane, so intent are they on bearing flowers, and seeds, for future generations.*

 Trying out new flowers and combinations is one of the pleasures of cottage gardening, and annuals make that easy. You might have had blue cornflowers last summer – why not have yellow marigolds this year, or even mix the two together? Annuals are favourites of parks departments, who plant them in formal rows and beds, but in a cottage garden you can set them in informal groups, mixing and matching with perennials and bulbs as your fancy takes you. With their long seasons of bloom, they fill in any gaps when other plants have retired from the stage or haven't yet begun their performance.

Annuals aren't expensive to buy. A tray of seedlings will cost you only a couple of pounds, and if you sow the seeds yourself you can have dozens of plants for even less money. Annuals are classed in two main groups: hardy annuals that can be sown directly in the ground in autumn or spring, and half-hardy annuals, often referred to as bedding, that are grown under cover and planted out when all danger of frost has passed. (Autumn sowing is rarely done, and if it is many will flower in early summer.)

As a general rule, annuals like sunshine and fertile soil (they have a lot to do in a short time) and, especially while they are young, they shouldn't be allowed to go short of water. Picking off spent blooms will encourage more flowers to grow and prolong the display. Keep a close watch for slugs and snails; caterpillars, too, can devastate seedlings.

Also included in this section are some traditional cottage garden favourites which are biennials. These take two years to complete their life-cycle, flowering and setting seed in their second year.

ALYSSUM
Lobularia maritima

The dwarf 'Carpet of Snow' is perhaps one of the best-known varieties. It forms a compact mass of white flowers 7.5–10cm (3–4in) high. The flowers have a soft, sweet scent of honey and butterflies adore them.

Sweet alyssum is the flower if you are in a hurry: the plants will often bloom six weeks after the seed is sown, which can be done *in situ* as soon as the ground is workable in spring. True, the individual flowers are tiny, but they grow in clusters that completely cover the plants and they have a sweet, honey scent. It is a hardy, spreading plant reaching 8–15cm (3–6in). Traditionally found in white or mauve forms, there are garden varieties in shades of pink, mauve, violet, and now apricot and cream. It is popular for edging paths and borders and container plantings, and in the rock garden. Use it too as a temporary ground cover around taller plants; white and mauve strains look very pretty beneath roses. The display should last for at least three months in summer and early autumn.

Alyssums often self-sow and, though self-sown plants tend to revert to white or mauve and to be taller than the named types, they are still very pretty. They will thrive in a sunny position in any well-drained soil.

The yellow alyssum or 'basket-of-gold' (*Aurinia saxatilis*) is a spring-flowering perennial with grey leaves and bright yellow flowers. It grows to about 20cm (8in) and needs sun and a well-drained soil.

BEGONIA
Begonia semperflorens

Wax begonias are often sold in mixed colours – but you can multiply your favourite colours by taking cuttings. Double-flowered cultivars are also available, but these cannot be propagated from seed.

Most of the many species and hybrids of this large genus are best treated as indoor or conservatory plants, but *B. semperflorens*, called the wax begonia for its waxy flowers and shining leaves, is a favourite garden flower. It is often planted in formal 'carpet bedding', but small clumps can look very well among other flowers, especially the varieties with bronze-tinted leaves that contrast well with their red, pink or white flowers, and it is an excellent plant for growing in containers.

Both the bronze-tinted and the green-leaved types flower for months – the Latin *semperflorens* means 'always flowering' – and, although we always think of them as annuals, they are in fact perennials which can live and bloom for two to three years in a frost-free climate. The bushy plants are usually about 15–30cm (6–12in) tall and the stems are very brittle, so plants should be positioned carefully where they won't get damaged.

Begonias like a rich, moist but well-drained soil and shelter from burning sun. They are valued for providing a colourful display in semi-shady areas but may become straggly and flower poorly in deep shade. They are difficult from seed, but can be bought as seedlings, plug plants or pot-grown plants.

BLANKET FLOWER
Gaillardia aristata

Here, blanket flowers are set against the red leaves of the dwarf dahlia 'Redskin'. Hot-coloured flowers look even richer when set against dark foliage.

There are both annual and perennial forms of this cheerful flower, and you should check which you are buying. The annuals are planted in spring to flower over a long summer season, the perennials in spring and summer to flower from late spring through summer. They are very similar and like the same conditions: full sun in well-drained soil. They do well in dry sandy soil and make excellent container plants.

They grow to 30–60cm (12–24in) and the daisy-like flowers can be either single or double (the double ones look like pompoms) and some have quilled petals; most annual strains are single. Deadhead regularly to prolong flowering. The blooms are excellent for cutting, too. They specialise in hot colours – red, yellow or orange – often weaving red and yellow in the one flower to give an effect like a Native American blanket. Hence the name – and they do come from America.

Their vibrant shades mean that these are not ideal flowers for lovers of the subtle, but they are great for jazzing up a summer planting, and they look particularly fine with blue or purple petunias or salvias.

CALIFORNIAN POPPY
Eschscholzia californica

The blue-green leaves of Californian poppies set off the orange blooms. Sow the seed in spring where they are to grow as these plants dislike being transplanted.

This difficult botanical name honours an Estonian botanist and explorer, but it is the only difficult thing about this lovely plant, the state flower of California. The early Spanish explorers called it *la calce d'oro*, the golden chalice, and that describes the flowers of the wild plant exactly: golden-orange bowls held on 30cm (12in) tall stems above the finely cut, bluish-green foliage.

However, plant breeders have created delightful variations on the theme — you can now have flowers in every warm shade from cream through yellow and orange to coral pink, and double-flowered varieties are available as well. The flowers tend to remain cup-shaped on dull days, but they open wide when there is bright sunshine.

This is one of the best and easiest of all flowers to grow in a dry, sunny situation, flowering from spring until autumn and needing little water. Any sort of soil suits it, so long as the drainage is perfect. Once you have the plant established, it will come up from self-sown seed for years — although these usually revert to the orange of the wild plants.

Sow seeds around blue lavender bushes, or set off its warm colours with the matching greyish foliage of herbs.

CANDYTUFT
Iberis

'Hyacinth-flowered' Iberis amara is set off well by Johnny-jump-ups (Viola tricolor). These will take over after the relatively short season of the candytuft is finished. The candytufts also make good cut flowers.

There are two distinct types of annual candytufts: those bred from *Iberis umbellata*, which grow up to 30cm (12in) tall at most and bear rounded clusters of small flowers in shades from white to cerise and crimson, and those developed from *I. amara*, which have slightly taller flower clusters, growing up to 60cm (24in). This second group is sometimes described as 'hyacinth-flowered', a bit of old-fashioned nursery hype rather than a fair comparison, and the blooms are usually white and scented. Both types are summer flowering. Autumn sowings give earlier blooms.

Candytufts are said to be the easiest of all flowers to grow from seed: just scatter the seeds in autumn or spring where the plants are to grow, and water them. There are no fads about soil or position.

The perennial candytufts — *I. sempervirens* and *I. saxatilis* — are prostrate plants for a well-drained position at a path edge or on top of a wall. They smother themselves with whiter-than-white flowers in late spring and early summer. Place them with care, however, as you may think their dazzling white blooms look a little stark among coloured flowers. The plants spread rapidly, making neat mats of evergreen foliage.

CANTERBURY BELLS
Campanula medium

A single white Canterbury bell grows here against a background of floss flower, with its contrasting colour and shape.

The Canterbury bell is one of a large and ornamental genus of widely differing plants. Its bell-shaped flowers come in cool pink and violet as well as the more usual blue or white, and it is grown as a biennial — most of the tribe are perennials. The flowers are carried on 60–90cm (24–36in) stems in late spring and early summer. Most popular are the double-flowered or 'cup and saucer' varieties (this describes the form of the flowers) but the plain single bells also have their admirers. All are lovely for cutting.

Although a biennial, if seed is sown in late winter under glass, and planted out in early spring, they will flower in the same year. Generally, seed is sown outdoors in midsummer to give flowers the following spring or summer. The plants like sun and a deep, rich soil, and snails adore them — take precautions as soon as you plant them out.

Because of their height they make excellent plants for the back of the border, and require little attention other than removing dead flowers to prolong the display. When the display finally fades, cut the whole plant back; there might just be a second lot of flowering stems if the weather is good.

CHINA ASTER
Callistephus chinensis

'Comet Mxd' is one of the lowest-growing strains to date, with little reduction in the size of the flowers. It is a natural partner for blue floss flower.

This is a lovely, old-fashioned flower, which is popular for growing as a massed planting in borders and in containers, and it is first rate for cutting too. If the foliage is a bit dull, the flowers are a delight: after many years of hybridising, they are now available in a wide range of eye-catching forms, including doubles, chrysanthemum-flowered, incurved, plumes and pompons, as well as the simpler, daisy-like forms. Sizes range from the dwarf, which grow to only 15cm (6in) tall, to the larger cultivars which will reach 60cm (24in) or more and will need support.

They flower in summer, and there are early, mid-season and late varieties, so plant a mixture or make successional sowings if you want a continuous display. Alternatively, concentrate on a late summer show alongside rudbeckias.

Sow the seed of China asters in early spring under glass, or outdoors in mid spring. Give them sun and rich soil. Don't plant them in the same place two years running as this increases the chances of their coming down with aster wilt, a fatal soil-borne fungus. Many current varieties are resistant to the fungus, but you don't want to tempt fate. Unfortunately, China asters are subject to some virus diseases, too.

CONVOLVULUS
Convolvulus

Roses can become bare at the base as they age. Convolvulus tricolor *will fill the gap and add a complementary colour.*

If your only experience of convolvulus is digging out the invasive white roots of the dreaded bindweed you may be a little wary of familiarising yourself with other varieties. You will, however, be missing out on some real treats. The annual forms include rapidly growing climbers, ideal to mix in with clematis, climbing roses and honeysuckles on rustic trellis or over shrubs. 'Star of Yelta' is rich blue with darker markings on the characteristic saucer-shaped blooms.

Convolvulus tricolor (*C. minor*) shows no inclination to climb and 'Ensign Mxd' is the best selection, with flowers in blue, rose and white and is also available as separate colours. Each bloom lasts just a day, but regular deadheading will keep them going for three months or more. Sow seed of these hardy annuals in the spring. To give climbers a flying start, start them off in March and April under glass in small pots. Varieties of *Convolvulus tricolor* can be sown directly into beds and borders in March and April.

Perhaps the most delectable of all bindweeds is the borderline hardy *C. sabatius* (syn. *C. mauritanicus*). It looks superb tumbling out of a tall terracotta jar or in hanging baskets. Young rooted cuttings are available for sale in the spring. It can also be grown from seed.

DIANTHUS
Dianthus chinensis & barbatus

Perfume and rich colour combinations make Sweet Williams an essential choice for the cottage border or vase.

As well as the familiar, much-loved cottage pinks and Sweet Williams, inseparable from the cottage garden and the larger border carnations, there are some mouth-watering varieties of dianthus that can be bought as pot-grown bedding just coming into bloom in the summer. These are ideal for filling gaps in containers and edging beds, as plants like pansies pass their prime. For larger quantities, grow your own from seed. They are all varieties of the Indian Pink, *Dianthus chinensis* and are dwarf, compact and prolific with flower colours as appetising as names like 'Strawberry Parfait' and 'Raspberry Parfait' suggest.

Sow seeds indoors in February and March for flowers from July until the frosts. Deadheading will ensure a continuous supply of blooms. They thrive in full sun or any well-drained soil but relish alkaline conditions. These dianthus will often survive outdoors for a year or two, but are at their most prolific in their first year.

Sweet Williams (*Dianthus barbatus*) can be raised from seed sown in summer to bloom the following May and June. Select blooms with a contrasting eye or ring for their old-fashioned charm.

CORNFLOWER
Centaurea cyanus

Purple and blue cornflowers with white roses make a cool, crisp colour scheme for early summer. There are few blue flowers that can match their intensity of colour: pink and red ones are also available.

The name 'cornflower' came from the abundance of this flower in the wheat fields of Europe, where the flowers shine against the ripening wheat; unfortunately, farmers' increasing use of herbicides has made this a rare sight now. The flower is sometimes called 'bachelor's buttons', from an ancient belief that if a young man puts one in his buttonhole and it lives, the lady he loves will return his affection; if it withers, she won't.

For all its romantic associations, this is a difficult flower to fit into a formal garden – the taller varieties are straggly in habit, and the season is short, only three weeks or so in late spring. But these are not really faults in a cottage-style planting. Just tuck in a few cornflowers among the other plants in the garden, and the others will both prop them up and keep the show going when the cornflowers fade.

Cornflowers are easy to grow, asking only for well-drained soil and sun. It is best to sow them *in situ*, in autumn or spring as soon as the ground is workable, as they do not like to be transplanted. It is also a good idea to make successional sowings at about two to three-week intervals to give a longer display of blooms, and sow an extra patch for cutting.

COSMOS
Cosmos bipinnatus

Cosmos are one of the easiest and best summer annuals to grow for cutting. They have tall stems and last well. Just seal the cut ends of the stems with a quick plunge in boiling water as soon as you have cut them.

Sometimes called the Mexican aster (they are indeed native to Mexico), the cosmos are both elegant and easy to cultivate. They vary in size from dwarf forms, growing to 45cm (18in), to tall varieties which make head-high bushy plants. They have airy, much divided (bipinnate) leaves and beautifully symmetrical flowers on long, graceful stems. The flowers come in various shades of crimson, pink and white. You can usually buy the white separately.

Cosmos sulphureus is quite distinct, growing 30–60cm (12–24in.) tall, and comes in a range of hotter colours – orange, red and bright yellow. Single colours are available or sow a mixture for some real border fireworks.

Their height makes the taller varieties of cosmos especially desirable plants for a new garden – they give an instant air of maturity – but tall flowers are useful in all gardens, to relieve any impression of flatness.

Cosmos like a hot, dry, sunny position in well-drained soil, where they will flower from midsummer until the first frosts. Sow the seeds (where the plants are to grow) in May or raise them in small pots and plant out when all danger of frost has passed. Taller forms will need staking. Both the flowers and the foliage are excellent for cutting.

FORGET-ME-NOT
Myosotis sylvatica

The tiny flowers of forget-me-not are the purest sky blue, each with a white and gold centre. The sticky seeds make them a nuisance beside paths but elsewhere they are delightful.

Romantics say the name was given because of the way some species grow on river banks: in folklore a knight of old fell into a torrent as he was picking some flowers for his lady and, as he was carried away by the current, he called out 'Forget me not!' The more cynical say it comes from the way the sticky seeds attach themselves to trouser legs and skirts as you brush by.

Forget-me-nots are low enough to be used as ground cover beneath spring bulbs and lush enough to distract the eye from the bulbs' post-flowering dying-off; and their colour goes with everything. (Pink and white varieties are available, too.)

Once forget-me-nots are established in your garden you will have them always as they self-seed very generously. In fact, the new plants follow the old so quickly that there is unlikely to be much bare soil for long. A shaded spot in moist soil suits them best.

To start forget-me-nots off, sow the seeds in midsummer; to keep them going, pull out the old plants when flowering is finally over, to make way for the new seedlings.

FOXGLOVE
Digitalis purpurea

White foxgloves are combined here with spires of blue delphiniums. The name foxglove is said to have been originally 'folks' glove', as it was said that fairies used to slip the bells over their fingers to keep them warm.

Foxgloves were long used in folk medicine to treat disorders of the heart and modern medicine still extracts valuable drugs from them for the same purpose. But don't try making your own home remedies: the plant is quite poisonous. Grow it for the early summer beauty of its 1.5m (5ft) spires of hanging bells, which come in a range of wonderful shades of purple, mauve, pink, apricot or white, all with purple spots in the throat.

These plants will grow in most soils, in sun or in shade, but they will do best in semi-shade and in a moist, fertile soil. Try growing them with an under-planting of blue forget-me-nots, with borage, which has similar foliage but flowers of a contrasting colour, or with old-fashioned roses, which are available in similar colours.

Foxgloves are short-lived perennials which are usually grown as annuals or biennials. The seed can be sown in summer outdoors or under glass in spring and planted out where they are to flower in September. Foxgloves will frequently come up from self-sown seed, but the white plants should be grown well away from the coloured ones or, after a couple of generations, you will find that all the flowers will be purple.

HOLLYHOCK
Alcea rosea

This annual strain of hollyhock produces single flowers that can become as large as those of a hibiscus. It is just as well worth growing as the double-flowered perennial strains.

With their wonderful tall spires of wide, circular flowers, hollyhocks can be a delightful sight, and they come in a beautiful range of warm colours: red, pink, yellow and white. The traditional annual cottage garden varieties are usually single, with flat circles of colour that look a little like their cousin the hibiscus, but some are double, with beautiful spheres of ruffled petals. All hollyhocks bloom in mid to late summer.

According to variety, traditional types can grow from 1.5m (5ft) tall to twice that. Modern shorter varieties have now been bred that do not need staking, which although more practical, perhaps do not have quite the same appeal as the towering stems of the older varieties.

Sow the seeds under glass in late winter, or outdoors in spring or summer for flowers the following year. The plants like the richest possible soil and sun and, although they need a sheltered spot where the top-heavy plants won't blow over in the wind, they should have plenty of fresh air or there could be trouble with rust, to which even the more disease-resistant modern strains are still rather prone. Plant are weakened but rarely killed; treat them as biennials, replacing old with new each year.

HONESTY
Lunaria annua

The soft purple of honesty's spring flowers combines well with other cool-toned blooms, such as these sweet peas. It also looks well with forget-me-nots, columbines or foxgloves.

Honesty is most familiar to us as the sprays of silvery, circular seed pods that appear so dramatically in dried flower arrangements, but the living plant is also a charmer, growing to 75cm (30in) and producing airy sprays of small mauve flowers in spring. There is a white variety too, and one with beautifully variegated leaves. Honesty is a lover of shade.

Once the plants have become fully established, they self-sow freely and come up from year to year. However, take care to keep the three types apart or they will cross and eventually the plain mauve will dominate. Otherwise, they need no special treatment: sow the seeds *in situ* in summer for flowers the following spring, and gather the sprays of seedheads for arrangements when they are ripe and pale brown.

The plants are not a fussy breed and will grow in most soils and positions, although they will do best in light, well-drained soil in a shady position.

The common name is said to have been given for the way the brown outer husks of the seed vessels fall as they ripen, to reveal the shiny, coin-like insides. The plant does not conceal its silver, you see.

LARKSPUR
Consolida ambigua

Larkspurs take their name from the short nectar-spur at the back of the flower, thought to resemble a bird's toe. The flowers come in shades of purple, lavender, pink and white as well as blue.

The larkspur used to be known as *Delphinium consolida*, and it is indeed a rather smaller version of the stately perennial delphiniums, bearing its flowers in upright spikes. A fast-growing annual, it flowers in early or midsummer. The taller, more widely grown forms produce their spikes of rounded, spurred flowers to 1.5m (5ft) in summer. The hyacinth-flowered larkspurs are lower-growing at 30–90cm (12–36in) and are earlier flowering. Larkspur has lacy, sometimes rather untidy foliage: it looks best with something lower in front. The colour range includes not only the blues and violets of its big cousins, but also pink and cerise.

Sow seed outdoors in spring, or in late autumn in mild areas for earlier flowers, and keep a few slim stakes handy as the plants are a bit top-heavy in flower. The blooms are first rate for cutting, and if you cut them when they are just opening, you can dry them.

The Chinese larkspur, *D. grandiflora*, syn. *D. chinense*, is a short-lived perennial usually grown as an annual, bearing brilliant deep blue flowers in loose branching spikes in summer. Grown in the same way as ordinary larkspur, it is a great plant for the front of the border.

LOBELIA
Lobelia erinus

The flowers of lobelias grown in the shade are less profuse but still very effective. They will self-sow quite happily if they like their position. Pinch out the growing tips of young plants to encourage bushiness.

Lobelias are amongst the most popular plants for the edges of bed, and pots and hanging baskets, where they will trail their colour out over the edge. They are frequently the most vivid, intense blue. The precise shade varies with the variety, from sapphire blue to the deep ultramarine of 'Crystal Palace', and there are whites and lilac pinks as well. Plants may be compact and bushy or trailing.

Everything about lobelia is on a small scale. It grows to only about 15cm (6in) tall, the leaves are tiny and the flowers barely half a centimetre wide: but these flowers come in such profusion from summer to autumn that the leaves are quite concealed for months.

Lobelia plants grow equally well in sun or light shade, although they do like moist, fertile soil: if they are starved flowering will be brief. (The usual rule of removing spent flowers can't be honoured: they are just too many and too small.) They can be grown from seed but as the seedlings take a long time to develop it is easier to buy plugs or young plants on the point of flower.

Quite different are the perennial lobelias from North America, which bear larger flowers on 60–90cm (2–3ft) tall spikes in summer and which are happiest in very moist, even boggy spots.

LOVE-IN-A-MIST
Nigella damascena

The sky-blue, double-flowered 'Miss Jekyll' is one of the most popular varieties. The lady after whom it was named pronounced her name quite unusually, to rhyme with 'treacle'.

The common name of this old cottage garden favourite comes from the way the flowers are half-hidden among the leaves. But the leaves are so fine and airy that the 5cm (2in) wide flowers still show up enough to be most effective in the summer garden. Perhaps the best known variety is the sky-blue 'Miss Jekyll', but strains are also available in mixtures of blue, lilac, pink and white, for example, 'Persian Jewels'.

The flowers are followed by oddly attractive, horned fruits that give the plant its alternative common name of 'devil-in-a-bush'. These are rather pretty when used in dried flower arrangements.

Love-in-a-mist grows up to about 60cm (24in), but the individual plants are rather flimsy in appearance, so that they look most pleasing in small groups among other flowers. A sunny position suits them best, in any good, well-cultivated soil.

Sow the seeds in autumn or in early spring, in the position where the plants are to grow as the plants dislike being transplanted. If the fruits are left to dry on the plants they will self-seed prolifically.

LUPIN
Lupinus

The annual lupins don't offer the brilliant shades of the perennial Russell hybrids, but they specialise in romantic pinks and blues for the spring garden, and some are fragrant too. They make excellent cut flowers.

Usually called *Lupinus hartwegii* in catalogues, the annual lupins are in fact hybrids derived from several species. They grow about 90cm (36in) tall and bear rather less stately, but still charming, flower spikes in soft shades of blue, mauve and pink. (Dwarf varieties, growing to only around 45cm (18in) or so, are available as well.)

Lupins are a delight with old-fashioned roses, but any flower of rounded habit would set them off very well. Californian poppies would be a good choice too, as they like the same conditions of sun and not too rich a soil.

Sow lupins in autumn or spring. Pick off the spent flower spikes to prolong the season, which should extend from midsummer into autumn.

The name *Lupinus* comes from the Latin *lupus*, meaning wolf: the Romans believed that lupins robbed the soil of fertility. In fact, the opposite of this is true as they are plants of the pea family which are able to 'fix' atmospheric nitrogen, and so when they die they leave the soil richer than before. They are thus among the best of plants for 'green manuring', the process of sowing a crop that will be cut down and dug into the soil at maturity, there to rot and add organic matter.

NASTURTIUM
Tropaeolum majus

This is not a fancy, named variety of nasturtium – just an old-fashioned, self-sown orange one. Nasturtiums are ideal plants for weekend houses or a wild garden as they don't want too much fuss made of them.

If nasturtiums were difficult plants to grow, gardeners would take them more seriously. Yet they are really very pretty, with their circular leaves and bright, pepper-scented flowers, available in every warm colour. They come in two types: the trailing varieties, which sprawl over a metre of ground or more and will make excellent, fast ground cover, particularly for dry banks where little else will grow, or will rapidly cover fences, and the compact types, which won't take over a mixed planting. There is even a variety with prettily variegated leaves called 'Alaska'.

The plants will grow in shady positions, but they will flower best in the sun. Don't plant them in rich soil, and don't over-water them, or abundant lush foliage will be produced at the expense of flowers. Sow the seeds, after all danger of frost has passed, where you want them to grow, as nasturtiums do not like to be transplanted.

This is a great plant for children's gardens, as the seeds are big and easy to handle – and both leaves and flowers are edible. In fact, they are tasty and nutritious, and can be added to salads. The unopened flower buds can be pickled as a substitute for capers.

ORNAMENTAL CABBAGE
Brassica oleracea

Nurseries often confuse the ornamental cabbage with its frillier relative, the kale. Colours intensify as the weather gets colder.

Nowadays you will no longer be thought eccentric if you grow cabbages in the front garden in the old cottage garden tradition of mixing flowers and vegetables, especially if you grow the fairly new ornamental cabbages. These make rosettes of leaves about 38cm (15in) wide, their cream or lilac and grey-green variegations making the plants look like immense flowers.

They are at their best in autumn and early winter when many other plants in the cottage garden have died back, and their colourful heads never fail to attract attention whether they are grown in the mixed border, as bedding, or as container plants. They will survive a mild winter and flower the following spring but it is the foliage that is the major feature. Ornamental kale is similar, with frillier leaves and is generally hardier.

These plants are as easy to grow as regular cabbages: sow the seeds in early summer, then transplant the young seedlings to a sunny spot. If there is a little lime in the soil, so much the better, but don't grow them in the same spot for several years for fear of the crippling cabbage disease club root. Being cabbages, they are edible but best reserved as a colourful garnish.

PANSY
Viola x *wittrockiana*

Traditionally pansies came in strong colours but in recent years softer tones have become popular. They are ideal in a cottage garden as there are colours to blend with almost anything.

Pansies are favourite plants for massing on their own, but they really look their best in the mixed company of the cottage garden. There, you can admire the flowers a few at a time. The shade from the other flowers will benefit them too, as in hot weather they can get small and spindly.

There are two types of pansy: those with black blotches forming the characteristic pansy 'face', which are pansies proper; and those with smaller, unblotched flowers, derived from *V. cornuta* (almost always called violas). Both come in almost every colour except real red, and there are now intermediate types in which the black blotches have been replaced with lighter colours. You can mix and match as you choose: the plants are available both in straight colours and as mixtures. Be careful to position the all-black one right at the front of the bed or you won't see it.

Although perennials, pansies are usually grown as annuals. In addition to the summer-flowering types, there are winter-flowering pansies which begin to bloom in late autumn and will continue through the winter in protected positions and peak in the spring. Plant pansies in sun or partial shade in a moist, fertile soil or grow in containers. Deadhead regularly to prolong flowering.

PETUNIA
Petunia

Petunia breeders like to produce matched sets of varieties: this one is also available in blue and salmon pink. Whether mass planted or tucked among other flowers, put them at the front of the bed to show off their colours.

Although petunias are highly bred and not typical of the cottage garden, the scent, colour and length of flowering make them invaluable to the modern cottage gardener. Use in moderation, surrounded by more authentic plants.

The flared, trumpet-shaped flowers come in just about every colour of the rainbow, available singly or in mixtures, some with markings, such as stripes, veins, stars and contrasting coloured edges. Flowers can be single or double; some have ruffled petals. The grandifloras have large flowers, up to 10cm (4in) across, but are often marked by rain and need protection. The multifloras are smaller, with flowers to only about 5cm (2in) across, but are more rain-resistant. Like the grandifloras, they have a delicious scent.

For a cascade of colourful, weather-resistant blooms, none can beat the surfinia petunias which shot to fame in the mid-1990s. These are vigorous, trailing plants which flower freely from mid-June to autumn, and are ideal for containers and ground cover.

Seed is sown under glass in early spring, but it is fine and tricky to raise, so most people buy seedlings, planting them in rich soil and sun. Deadhead regularly and cut back hard if the plants become straggly.

PINCUSHION
Scabiosa atropurpurea

The long stems and rich colours – pinks and crimsons as well as blue – of pincushions make them delightful cut flowers.

This is another genus with both annual and perennial species. The annuals, derived from *Scabiosa atropurpurea*, don't bloom for quite as long as the perennials but they are very pretty, easily-grown flowers for summer and autumn, and are good for cutting. They are available in a very pleasing range of cool colours – blue, mauve, pink, white – and carmine.

They have rather pleasant, fuzzy leaves and, although some grow to 90cm (36in), they rarely need staking. Dwarf forms are also available. Sow the seed in spring where the plants are to grow. They like sun but aren't fussy about soil. The annual drumstick scabious or 'papermoon', *S. stellata*, is grown for its unusual spherical seedheads.

The perennials are mainly blues and mauves, ranging in height from about 20cm (8in) to 90cm (36in). They flower in summer and autumn.

The common name comes from the flowerheads, in which the stamens stand out from the flowers, just like pins in a pincushion. The rather off-putting scientific name derives from the use of the plant in folk medicine as a cure for the itch, alias scabies.

POPPY
Papaver

The Iceland poppy has softly scented flowers on long slim stems. These are just two of its harmonious colours. Unlike most poppies, the flowers can be used for cutting as they last well in water.

The poppies are a large tribe, including both rare and difficult flowers as well as many that are both popular and easy to grow. Two of the most important annual species are the corn poppy and the Iceland poppy.

The corn poppy, *P. rhoeas*, grows in the cornfields of Europe with the cornflower, and the combination of cornflower blue and poppy scarlet is effective in the garden, too. If you find the wild plant too brilliant for your garden, try the Shirley poppies, which come in much more refined shades of pink to white. There are also beautiful double-flowered Shirleys. All types grow to about 60cm (24in) and flower in summer.

The Iceland poppy, *P. nudicaule*, makes low tufts of fresh green leaves, from which the flowers rise on 30cm (12in) stems. This is a popular poppy, with fragrant single blooms. Many different colour forms have been selected, and the sunset tones of the mixtures are very harmonious.

Poppies can be grown from seed sown in the autumn or the spring and all like sun and fertile soil. The Iceland poppy is a bit tricky to raise, so most people buy seedlings. The others mentioned are easy to grow and are best sown where they are to flower.

POT MARIGOLD
Calendula officinalis

The bright orange flowers of pot marigold are not only decorative in the garden, they can be used to make a colourful addition to salads, butters and cheeses and cooked dishes such as omelettes and soups.

No wonder these obliging hardy annuals were amongst the cottagers' favourites. They are bright and breezy with fresh orange or yellow petals appearing from May to the frosts and they will self-seed from one year to the next without ever becoming a nuisance. The petals make a colourful addition to drinks and salads, a characteristic shared with a perfect planting partner for them in the garden – borage, which has delightful star-shaped blue flowers.

Plant breeders have done a lot of work on Calendula and come up with dwarfer more densely flowering varieties that still have the character and charm of the humble pot marigold. 'Fiesta Gitana Mxd' is an outstanding dwarf double. For cutting and garden display 'Kablouna Mxd' has stunning, crested blooms and grows up to 20in (50cm) tall. 'Touch of Red Mxd' has petals burnished in red and includes a pale biscuit-apricot shade that is quite a departure from the usual yellow and orange.

For really early blooms, sow pot marigolds in beds and borders in September to start into flower from May onwards the following year. They will also make a welcome early flowering pot plant for a cold greenhouse. Alternatively, sow indoors in March or directly into the garden in April and May.

SNAPDRAGON
Antirrhinum majus

Compact strains of snapdragon like 'Magic Carpet Mxd' can be as short as 15cm (6in). There are also now strains with open, bell-shaped flowers and double ones.

In recent years plant breeders have been busy developing dwarf and compact varieties of snapdragon, which are supposedly more suited to the small modern garden than the traditional tall varieties. But surely the whole point of a snapdragon is the superb elegance of its long-stemmed spikes of flowers? True, the foliage isn't noteworthy, but in a cottage garden planting it is easy to mask this with other plants.

Check what sort of flower you are getting: the new strains are not necessarily an improvement over the old-fashioned, two-lipped flowers, loved by children who open them up to see the stamens inside.

You can sow the seeds either in late summer, and overwinter them in a cold-frame, for a spring display, or in spring, when the plants will start to flower in midsummer. They like rich soil and at least a half day of sun. When the flowers fade, cut the plants back and give them some fertiliser and they will stage a repeat performance. Their biggest worry is snapdragon rust. Happily, most of the current strains are fairly resistant, but you should spray with a fungicide if you see any signs. It is worst in wet summers.

SPIDER FLOWER
Cleome spinosa

Of the many plants known as spider flowers, C. spinosa is as handsome as any. Keep the plants bushy by pinching back the tips.

Even though it is a half-hardy annual, a plant of the spider flower in full bloom has all the bulk and air of permanence of a flowering shrub. It is easy to grow, too. Sow seeds under glass in spring and plant out in early summer in rich, well-drained soil: the plants will rapidly create bushes 90–120cm (3–4ft) tall and nearly as wide, each branch crowned with a head of flowers. The display will continue from summer to autumn.

Amongst the best-known varieties are 'Pink Queen', with pale pink flowers, and 'Helen Campbell' with white flowers: but there are also strains available in mixed shades of pink, mauve and white. As the flower stems elongate, the thin seed pods grow horizontally beneath the flowers, and it is these that give the plant its common name. Try putting three plants on their own in a large terracotta pot or use them to back up Michaelmas daisies or mingle seductively with tall cosmos.

These tropical plants which originate from South and Central America, grow best if they are given a sunny position with fairly rich soil.

SWEET PEA
Lathyrus odoratus

Sweet peas are beautiful, long-lasting cut flowers and a bunch of them will fill the room with fragrance. There are also perennial species which are just as beautiful but they lack the wonderful fragrance of L. odoratus. Most common is the climber L. latifolius, which has flowers in shades of cerise, pink or white in summer and early autumn.

Sweet peas are most admired for their delicious perfume, but are also grown for their stems of multiple ruffled blooms in a range of colours – pink, red, blue, white and cream.

They need support but there is no need to confine them to climbing on walls and fences. You can, for instance, make a teepee of three or four tall slender stakes (bamboo would be perfect) and grow a half-dozen or so plants on it to make a pillar of flowers. Or you could select one of the 'bush' varieties that grow into rather floppy bushes about 30–60cm (12–24in) tall and place it just as you would any other annual. Try them at the top of a retaining wall, where they can trail over the edge.

Lathyrus odoratus is not the only sweet pea worth growing. Consider the perennial climber, *L. latifolius*, the everlasting pea, which dies down for the winter and in summer bears lovely but scentless flowers on stems that grow to 2m (6ft 6in) or more.

Make sure sweet pea plants get plenty of sunshine and the richest possible soil. Sow the seeds in autumn, or under glass in late winter, first soaking them overnight in warm water to speed germination.

Sweet peas will continue to flower throughout summer, provided you regularly pick off the spent flowers to prevent the plants going to seed. Don't ever try to divide sweet peas as they hate it.

VIRGINIAN STOCK
Malcolmia maritima

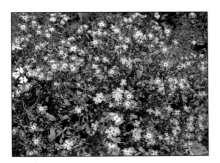

Each four-petalled Virginian stock flower is beautifully shaded and veined, with a delicate scent. It was a very popular flower in colonial America – hence its common name.

The Virginian stock is the perfect flower for lovers of the dainty. It grows to only about 20cm (8in) tall, and so one plant may seem a little insubstantial, despite the prettiness of its delicately scented flowers. But sow a quantity of them, in front of and around taller flowers and in front of shrubs, and they will quickly create a carpet of softly scented, four-petalled stars in a very pleasing blend of mauves, red, cool pinks and white.

These plants are just the thing for carpeting a bed of old-fashioned roses, or for filling in around clumps of herbs. Another bonus is the speed at which Virginian stocks grow – the first flowers can appear only six weeks or so after the seeds are sown.

Sow the seed in early autumn for spring flowers, and continue to sow in succession from spring onwards to give a long flowering season from spring to autumn. The Virginian stock prefers a sunny position in fertile, well-drained soil and will often appear from self-sown seed.

The scientific name honours William Malcolm, a Scottish nurseryman of the early nineteenth century.

WALLFLOWER
Cheiranthus cheiri

Double-flowered wallflowers have been known since the sixteenth century, and became very fashionable in Victorian times when choice forms had to be grown from cuttings, but seed strains that produce a high percentage of doubles are now available. There is still room for improvement, however. Seed-grown strains are not always very uniform in habit. Try selecting the ones that impress you most and take cuttings of the unflowered shoots in spring.

Still the most popular spring bedding plant by far, the wallflower takes its name from the wild wallflowers that grow on ruined castles in Europe, but in gardens they should be given better fare than rubble. Give them sun and fertile soil and they will make bushy plants and cover themselves in late spring with short spikes of flowers. They come in a range of warm toned colours, including yellow, cream, bronze, copper-red and pink, and have a distinctive spicy fragrance all their own.

Most people find the single-flowered types the most attractive. There are many old-fashioned double-flowered forms which have been known since the sixteenth century, but these can be a little shapeless. As a result of modern breeding, however, some good forms are now becoming available.

There are tall varieties which grow to 60cm (24in) and dwarf varieties which reach only about 20cm (8in) and are better for more exposed positions and for pots and windowboxes. 'Prince Mixed' is an outstanding dwarf strain.

Wallflowers like a bit of lime in the soil and should be sown in early summer so that the plants will be as big as possible before winter. Wallflowers transplant quite easily and you can grow them on through the summer in a nursery bed, and then transplant them (with due care) to their final positions in late summer to early autumn.

The closely-related erysimums tend to be smaller and are more suitable for the rock garden and the front of the border. Some wallflowers once classified as cheiranthus are now classed as erysimum.

ZINNIA
Zinnia

The varieties of Z. haageana feature two-toned flowers, either single or double. They are rather smaller than the Z. elegans cultivars, both in the size of the flowers (about 4–5cm/ 1.5–2in) and the height of the plant.

The zinnia comes from Mexico and it is said the Aztecs used to sprinkle the young plants with blood to intensify their colour. There is no need to do that: the scarlet, gold, magenta or shocking pink of these summer annuals is already bright enough for most people.

The plants are rather stiff bushes and, although they are favourites for massing in large beds, they really look their best in a cottage garden, set in small clumps among and behind other, quieter plants. Try them with lavender or catmint to cool them down, or turn up the heat by planting them with dwarf strawflowers (Helichrysum).

If you find the usual varieties a bit brash, you can buy all-white strains and a very attractive variety, called 'Envy', with lime-green flowers. Then there are the lower-growing varieties of *Z. haageana*, such as 'Old Mexico' and 'Persian Carpet'. These grow to 25–30cm (10–12in), as against the 60–90cm (24–36in) height of the usual strains, and are much daintier with smaller flowers in unusual shades of mahogany and gold.

All the zinnias are good for cutting, and all are easy to grow. Sow the seeds *in situ* in late spring, and give the plants fertile soil and plenty of sunshine. No climate is too hot for them. The plants are free-flowering and the blooms are weather-resistant.

Keep dead flowers snipped off to prolong their flowering and the display will last from midsummer through to autumn. Watch the young seedlings carefully as snails love them.

*P*ERENNIALS *are the*

mainstay of most cottage garden borders, offering the gardener a wonderful range of flowers and foliage for all seasons.

 Perennials can be considered as more or less permanent features in the garden as the rootstock remains, even though many of them die back each winter, replacing their top growth with fresh new shoots each season.

Perennials might at first seem expensive to buy when compared to annuals, but their long-lasting nature means that they really are excellent value in the long term, and their clumpy habit makes them among the easiest of all plants to propagate, perhaps swapping a division or two with a friend as you do so. In most cases all you need to do is simply dig up a clump at the appropriate season and divide it into several new plants, which should be replanted immediately in the garden, or potted up to be passed on to friends and neighbours.

At the same time as you propagate them, you can also take the opportunity to rearrange your plants and vary your garden design: while they may be long-lasting plants, perennials don't need to be seen as features that are fixed in position, in the same way as shrubs and trees.

It is always a good idea to blend annuals and perennials. While you wait for your perennials to clump up you can fill in the gaps in the beds and borders with annuals. Also, most perennials don't flower for more than a few weeks, leaving the annuals to fill out the seasons with colour.

As a general rule, perennials need at least a half day of sunshine and most of them will appreciate well-drained soil that has been enriched with compost or well-rotted manure before planting. (After all, they are going to perform for years in the same bed.)

Don't be in too much of a hurry to divide your plants unless you want to increase your stock. If a clump is flowering happily, leave it in peace; however, if it seems to be getting overcrowded and you find that flowering is declining, then it is time to divide it up and replant the various sections.

ACHILLEA
Achillea

The flat yellow flowerheads of Achillea millefolium *'Moonshine' are borne throughout summer above the feathery grey-green leaves. They look particularly well mingled with blue and purple flowers.*

With its distinctive, flat-topped yellow flowerheads, *Achillea filipendula* is doubly valuable, both for border display to contrast with blooms such as the erect blue spikes of *Salvia* x *superba* or delphiniums and as a long-lasting cut flower that can also be dried for winter arrangements.

'Gold Plate' is the classic form and also the tallest at 1.2–1.5m (48–60in). 'Coronation Gold', which is more suited to narrow borders at 60cm (24in) high, flowers from June to August. 'Moonshine' is a similar height, but its ferny leaves are noticeably greyer. With purple sage it contrasts in both leaf and bloom (blue with yellow).

Our native yarrow (*A. millefolium*) has produced some refined selections, such as 'Fireking'. 'Summer Pastels Mxd' produces a beautiful colour range of apricot, salmon, scarlet, lilac, cream, orange, white and gold that can be easily grown from seed. From an early sowing in February you can expect flowers in the first year.

Achillea ptarmica 'The Pearl' has daisy buttonheads and a running habit that suits jumbled cottage borders. Achilleas can be divided every three years to increase your stock.

ASTER
Aster

Aster x frikartii *is a top ten perennial and mixes in wonderfully with sedums like this 'Autumn Joy'.*

Just as your borders are getting a little ragged with some summer performers beginning to flag, out pop the Michaelmas daisies to signal that autumn is on the way. Their simple daisy flowers are the perfect complement for other cottage garden perennials like sedum, Japanese anemones and Chinese lanterns. The colour range is limited to purple, mauve, lilac and violet, with an occasional white and pale yellow, particularly amongst the smaller-flowered types such as *A. ericoides*.

Even the most enthusiastic grower would not deny the fact that many Michaelmas daisies are prone to powdery mildew, particularly in dry, starved soils and *A. novi-belgii* varieties will inevitably succumb without regular spraying with a fungicide.

However, there are some outstanding varieties that are mildew-resistant, such as *Aster* x *frikartii* with its orange-centred blue flowers borne right through from late July to October. For the front of a border or pots, *A. thompsonii* 'Nanus' is a delight in lavender blue. *A. amellus* varieties like 'Violet Queen' are well worth considering, as are the New England asters, particularly the purple-red *A. novae-angliae* 'Andenken an Alma Potschke'.

ASTILBE
Astilbe

The hardy Fuchsia 'Mrs Popple' makes an unconventional but pleasing partner for red and pink astilbes.

Plants with attractive leaves and flowers have to be doubly valuable to the gardener and the astilbes are blessed with both. Their leaves often emerge in the spring with red or bronze tints and are then followed by thrusting spikes of fluffy flowers.

Given a soil that doesn't dry out they will thrive in sun as well as being a clever choice for that wet sticky patch in shade. In fact they look superb growing on the wet margins of ponds and streams. Good planting partners include hostas, primulas and daylilies. The dead flower spikes have a modest beauty if spared the secateurs in the autumn.

'Bressingham Beauty' is a robust tall clear pink variety with spikes to about 90cm (36in). 'Fanal' is a popular hot crimson red, while 'Irrlicht' is a cool white with dark leaves. Good dwarf varieties include *A. chinensis* var. *pumila*, which has bright rose-purple spikes reaching 30cm (12in) and the even smaller *A. simplicifolia* 'Sprite' which is like a miniature version of the taller hybrids. Plants can be bought and planted from containers throughout the year, even when they are in flower.

ASTRANTIA
Astrantia major

Astrantia 'Hadspen Blood' is one of the most richly-coloured and also one of the most sought-after varieties. Plant it amongst catmint for contrast.

There is a modest and old-fashioned charm to astrantia flowers, a fact borne out by common names like Hattie's Pincushion, though those in search of spectacular blooms might find them a little lacking in impact. Close inspection, however, reveals a fascinating flower in shades of red and pink as well as the more usual white. The tiny true flowers are surrounded by bracts which give them an intricate lace-like quality and, as you'd expect, they last very well as a cut flower.

Astrantias will grow in sun or shade in any reasonable soil and are at their best in June and July though flowers will continue to appear intermittently until the autumn. *Astrantia major* 'Sunningdale Variegated' has the added bonus of leaves handsomely marked with yellow and cream. 'Hadspen Blood', a recent introduction, is one of the best reds and looks most striking with hardy pink geraniums like 'Wargrave Pink' and variegated hostas. 'Shaggy' has an enlarged collar of bracts around the flower making it a real conversation piece.

Astrantias can be grown from seed sown in the autumn or in spring if pre-chilled in the fridge for six weeks prior to sowing. Named varieties can be bought and planted throughout the year.

AUBRIETA
Aubrieta

As a change from yellow alyssum, try aubrieta with red ornamental quince and yellow variegated euonymus.

Even reluctant gardeners are familiar with the purple and blue trailing mound-forming aubrieta so often seen running freely alongside yellow alyssum and white arabis over rocks and path edges. Common it may be, but it has the perfect habit and constitution to soften and clothe the hard lines of walls and paving, an important consideration in creating the comfortable care-free style of the cottage garden.

Full sun and good drainage are all that are required. Aubrieta even thrive in limey soils, though, like most plants, they respond to a little extra care. Plants that are trimmed back after flowering with shears will produce much more compact and bushy plants. Old neglected plants, in contrast, tend to become thin and straggly.

Named varieties will prove superior to cheaper seed-raised mixtures often sold as spring bedding plants in autumn and spring. 'Dr. Mules' is a robust old favourite with double purple flowers. 'Red Carpet' is a stronger shade. There are also some attractive variegated varieties, 'Argenteovariegata' being particularly noteworthy. All aubrietas can be propagated from cuttings taken in the summer and autumn.

CAMPANULA
Campanula

Campanula glomerata 'Superba' spreads quickly to cover the poorest soils with rich, violet-blue heads of bloom up to 60cm (24in) high.

Few gardeners fail to come across bellflowers whether in the border, rock garden, in pots or self-sown between crevices in paving and on gravel paths. There are more than 300 campanulas, many hardy perennials, others annuals or biennials, and although pinks and whites appear regularly, it is the pale or deep blues that are most associated with this genus.

Campanulas are great mixers, making soothing go-betweens amongst shrub roses, and the lower, spreading alpine varieties such as *C. portenschlagiana* look a treat with pinks. For wide borders where height is needed, choose varieties like *C. latifolia* that grow to about 1.2m (48in). 'Brantwood' is rich violet-purple; 'Gloaming' is another gem with pale mauve bells. 'Prichard's Variety' is the most familiar variety of *C. lactiflora*, again tall, reaching 90cm (36in), and a violet blue that looks wonderful with lilies. 'Loddon Anna' represents the pink end of the spectrum.

Campanula persicifolia 'Telham Beauty' is a seductive pale blue; the sort of plant that no gardener should be deprived of. Altogether a classic bellflower for the archetypal cottage border.

COLUMBINE
Aquilegia hybrids

The old-fashioned A. vulgaris *specialises in cool colours. There is something bird-like in the way the flowers flutter on their slender stems: the common name comes from the Latin* columba, *a dove, Aquilegia from Latin* aquila, *an eagle.*

There are two main types of columbine grown in the cottage garden: the old-fashioned granny's bonnets (*Aquilegia vulgaris*), which come in cool tones of pinks and blues as well as purples and white and have short, curled-up nectar-spurs; and the glamorous long-spurred hybrids, more lightly built in plant and foliage, with flowers in just about every colour you can think of. It is sometimes possible to buy plants in single colours, but they cross very readily and mixtures are more usual.

Both types of aquilegia grow to around 60–90cm (2–3ft) high, sometimes taller or shorter, and flower in late spring and early summer. The season is fairly brief but it can be extended by regularly pinching off the spent flowers to encourage the development of more blooms. The foliage is attractive all summer, and gold-leaved and variegated forms are available.

Aquilegias are not long lived plants but they will often come up from self-sown seed. Give them a well-drained soil in an open, sunny site for the best results. They can be divided in autumn, but you will get stronger plants from seed sown in autumn or spring. Seed from mixed plantings will, however, not come true to type.

CORAL BELLS
Heuchera sanguinea

Coral bells here line a path, a use for which they are ideally suited. The airy summer flowers won't hide anything growing behind, and the ground-hugging foliage is neat and attractive all summer.

Although coral bells can grow as high as half a metre tall when they are in bloom in summer, they are still a good choice for the front of a planting – the flower sprays are so light and airy that they scarcely hide what might be growing behind them. The round evergreen leaves, which grow in neat tufts close to the ground, are a pretty finish to a bed in their own right. The flowers are tiny bells, borne on many-branched stalks that match them in colour, and last well when cut.

There are several varieties available, in various shades of carmine, coral or pink: and while they are not always individually named they are all very pretty. The variety 'Palace Purple' has purple-toned leaves and pale flowers, and several new foliage varieties have recently been introduced, including those with satiny-silvery or purple leaves or ruffled foliage.

Coral bells do best in lightly shaded positions, and the colour of the flowers tends to hold better there. The plants appreciate a soil that is moisture-retentive but well-drained, and should be divided and replanted every three years or so: they rapidly form clumps and become overcrowded. Spring is the best time to divide them.

CRANESBILL
Geranium

Cool down the extrovert magenta red blooms of Geranium psilostemon *by letting them run through a blue-flowered variety.*

The cranesbills or hardy geraniums make up a rich and varied group of plants. (The name 'cranesbill' comes from the pointed seed vessels.) They are hardy and easy to grow, with a wide variety of leaf shapes and textures and flowers in shades of pink, purple and blue, as well as white. Most hardy geraniums flower in summer.

The following are amongst the many species to choose from: *G. sanguineum*, called the bloody cranesbill for the red sap of the roots, which has magenta or clear pink flowers in summer; *G. pratense*, the meadow cranesbill, a native British plant with tall heads of violet-blue flowers and deeply-cut foliage, and its many forms; *G. grandiflorum*, in several forms, some with soft blue flowers; *G. phaeum*, the mourning widow, with pretty leaves and small, almost-black flowers; and *G. macrorrhizum*, one of the best ground-cover plants for shade, which has pale pink or white flowers; and many hybrids.

None is at all difficult or fussy about soil as long as it is not waterlogged, and most prefer sun, although some do better in shade. Propagation is by division in autumn or spring.

DAHLIA
Dahlia pinnata x *D. coccinea*

Dahlias come in a range of sizes, from enormous to rose-sized. All are first-rate cut flowers, lasting best if you cut them young and pass the cut ends of the stems quickly through a candle flame to seal them.

Dahlias are the ideal plants for the back of a mixed planting, where their height (they can grow up to 2m (7ft) tall) won't swamp their neighbours. Enthusiasts take a lot of trouble with them, dividing clumps of tubers with care, pinching and pruning the bushes and thinning the buds to ensure the largest, most perfect flowers on long stems.

For a bright show in the garden, however, all you need to do is plant the sprouted tubers in late spring in rich, well-drained soil, pinch back the developing plants 3–4 weeks after planting to make them bushy, and stake them to keep them from collapsing. They will then bloom from just after midsummer until the first frost cuts them down. The only essential is sunshine: the plants won't flower in shade. Any good soil suits, especially if rich and generously watered.

Keep the spent flowers picked off, both for neatness and to encourage more to follow. Lift the tubers each autumn, trim off the top growth, dry them and store them in a dry, frost-free place.

There is a seemingly infinite variety of types. There are the giant decoratives, with shaggy flowers the size of dinner plates; the more refined nymphaea or water-lily-flowered varieties; the pompons, with perfect spheres of petals the size of golf balls; the collarettes, which have single flowers with a contrasting ruff at the centre; and, most popular of all, the cactus dahlias. The dwarf bedding dahlias, usually grown from seed, need no staking as they grow only about 30–50cm (12–20in) tall. They have smallish flowers that are usually single or semi-double. Patio dahlias are relatively new, with larger blooms on compact bushes. All varieties come in just about every colour you can imagine except blue, and are always clean and pure: they never clash with each other.

DAYLILY
Hemerocallis hybrids

Cream flowers like this one are the closest breeders have come in their quest for the white daylily. That is no great disappointment, as pale cream is not a common colour in flowers and it is a useful one in the garden – it can be used to separate clashing tones where white would be too sharp a contrast.

The daylily was once considered 'old-fashioned', and indeed it has been around for quite a while, but the rather ordinary species and old garden types that were originally grown have been joined over the past forty years or so by an extensive range of hybrids.

The colour range has been extended to include just about every warm colour, but not blue. Daylilies are now available in yellow, orange, salmon pink, mauve, red (often rather russet-tinted) and beige and tawny tones that can only be matched by chrysanthemums. The lily-like flowers often display contrasting colours in their throats.

There are many specialist nurseries that now list hundreds of named varieties, often with startlingly high prices attached to the latest imports. Daylily lovers long for a white variety but so far cream is the best that breeders have been able to achieve.

All are first-rate garden plants, with attractive grassy foliage and many flower stems, which can grow from 45cm (18in) to about 90cm (36in), according to variety. They are strong enough not to need staking. The individual flowers last only a day – hence the name daylily – but the best varieties produce them in an unending succession throughout the summer. Some daylilies, although not all, are quite delicately scented in the evening.

Daylilies do best in fertile soil in full sun, but they will grow in light shade, and although they love moisture they are surprisingly drought-resistant. Take care to protect the young foliage from the attentions of slugs and snails as it emerges in the spring.

Propagate named varieties by division in autumn or spring, as cultivars raised from seed will not come true to type. Late autumn is the best planting time and once they are established the plants will make big clumps that can be left undisturbed for years.

DORONICUM
Doronicum

The bold yellow daisies of Doronicum orientale *are almost inseparable from the spring cottage border.*

The first daisy perennial flower of the spring, it is hard to imagine a cottage garden without a respectable clump or two of these obliging flowers alongside elephant ears (bergenia). Can you imagine a posy of spring flowers that doesn't include a single or double doronicum among the grape hyacinths and wallflowers?

Doronicum or leopard's bane is easy and trouble-free in sun or shade; slugs are likely to be the only cause of trouble before the foliage is fully expanded. 'Spring Beauty' is a popular double to 45cm (18in) tall, but lacks the charm of the singles like 'Harper Crewe'. Another single, 'Miss Mason', has an award of merit so is well worth tracking down.

Deadheading will often encourage a second flush of flowers in late spring or autumn. Try doronicums among drifts of blue lungwort and green-flowered hellebores (*H. argutifolius*) with orange-centred daffodils.

Divide established clumps every three years or so between October and March when they are dormant or just coming into growth. Like many herbaceous perennials, they can be bought in containers throughout the year, in small 9cm (3in) pots or as larger clumps.

ECHINACEA
Echinacea purpurea

The bristly central boss of the cone flower expands and becomes more prominent as it ages.

If you're not familiar with the purple cone flower, the first thing you notice is the sheer size of the flowers. These North American daisies produce monster blooms, particularly on young vigorous plants. Imagine an out-sized rudbeckia and you're close, although the prominent boss of stamens forms an even more pronounced cone in echinacea.

The most widely grown variety is *E. purpurea* 'The King'; crimson-pink with a mahogany centre. The stems are stout and the leaves luxuriant and glossy. 'Robert Bloom' is a similar height 90–120cm (36–48in) with purple rose flowers, while 'White Swan' has white petals and an orange-brown centre.

Given full sun and soil enriched with well-rotted manure or garden compost, purple cone flowers will flower from July through to October. Deadheading will prevent seeds forming which can curb further flowering, but to keep things tidy, remove lengths of stem at the same time.

You can increase your stock of echinacea by chopping up short lengths of root in February and growing them on in a peat and sand mixture or by division at the same time. Seed is available of named varieties as well as of mixed hybrids, and plants can be bought in containers throughout the year.

EUPHORBIA
Euphorbia species

The tall Euphorbia characias ssp. wulfenii *has strong architectural qualities and will make a bold statement in any border display.*

There's no doubting the popularity of the spurges with gardeners who value the sculptural qualities particularly evident in the taller sub-shrubby species like *E. characias* subsp. *wulfenii* and the carpeting *E. myrsinites*. Habit is very variable, but all have the characteristic green, yellow or red bracts that surround the true flowers which are small and insignificant. As with astrantias and hellebores, their flower structure gives them the ability to look decorative for weeks.

For effective ground cover even in dry shade, *E. amygdaloides* var. *robbiae* is outstanding and evergreen with yellow-green bracts in spring and looks lovely with daffodils. *E. polychroma* will add a patch of sunshine to cottage beds and borders and looks a picture under red-flowered ornamental quince. You can reverse this colour scheme by planting the red 'Fireglow' with yellow doronicum. For trailing over walls and rocks, the grey-leaved *E. myrsinites* is a treasure and never better than when planted with grape hyacinths. If you can cope with its running habit, the cypress spurge (*E. cyparissias*) will mingle with bulbs and early perennials. Cut back spurges when they're past their prime, but wear gloves and goggles to avoid the caustic white sap.

DELPHINIUM
Delphinium elatum

'Pacific Giant' delphiniums grow head-high and come in just about every shade of blue and purple imaginable. The massive flower spikes are ideal for a cottage garden, where the spires of bloom rise above lower flowers.

Delphiniums are not the easiest of plants but they do look their best in a cottage garden where they can raise their spires of bloom above less stately flowers in summer. With colours from white through mauve and sky blue to pure deep blue and violet, they go happily with almost anything. Roses are favourite companions.

The tallest varieties may reach a height of 2.5m (8ft), but there are smaller-growing varieties reaching only 1–1.35m (3–4.5ft). The named varieties that are one of the glories of an English summer don't travel well, and the rest of the world relies on the American-bred 'Pacific Giants' strain, or the Belladonnas, which have graceful sprays about a metre tall.

The secrets of growing delphiniums are not difficult, and there are four: a little afternoon shade; the richest, well-drained soil you can manage; constant protection from snails; and plenty of water from the time the new growth starts in early spring until the flowers are over. The flower spikes will almost certainly need staking.

After they fade, cut off the old spikes, apply fertiliser and keep watering. They will almost always stage a scaled-down repeat performance.

GAURA
Gaura lindheimeri

The scientific name Gaura, mock-Greek for 'superb' and 'decorative', is short and to the point. Shown here in early summer, the flower stems will later branch and grow longer, laden with clouds of white blossom.

This elegant flower is a lovely sight in full bloom, its hundreds of dainty white flowers fluttering on almost invisibly fine stems like so many white butterflies. The display lasts throughout the summer, growing ever more delightful as the flower stems branch and then branch and branch again. In full flight, the plant will be rather more than 1m (3ft) tall, with each of the blossoms being about 2.5cm (1in) wide.

For all its grace, this is not a plant for a starring role – set it in among other, bolder flowers, as you would use small delicate flowers in a flower arrangement. Place it a little back from the front so other plants will mask its foliage, which is mid-green and lance-shaped and rather ordinary. Try it in an all white scheme or use its clouds of white flowers to make peace between clashing colours. It also looks effective when mass planted.

Gaura prefers full sun and light, well-drained soil, although the flowers will be most lavish if the plant isn't starved. Pinch back the first shoots in spring to encourage more flower stems and, if the plant gets straggly cut it back hard – it will respond with new growth. As plants tend to be short-lived, propagate by semi-ripe cuttings in summer, or seed sown in autumn or spring.

GAZANIA
Gazania rigens

Gazanias are sometimes called treasure flowers, an apt name for their jewel-bright colours, often set off with gold. Their only fault is they won't open on dull days or in the shade.

These attractive perennials are only half-hardy, and except in the mildest areas they are best grown as annuals. They form ever-widening carpets of evergreen leaves, usually dull, dark green with silver undersides but sometimes all silver or grey, adorned for months on end with flowers in sunshine colours. The range is extraordinary – from a packet of seed you can expect cream, yellow, orange, russet and coral, with most flowers having touches of black at the centre and many being striped in contrasting tones.

Their love of poor, sandy soil and resistance to drought makes gazanias ideal for a seaside garden, and their low growth means that the sea wind doesn't bother them. But they are just as useful inland, too. They are great for edging a path and love to spread over paving. In a mixed planting you may need to watch their tendency to spread into their neighbours, but they are easy to keep under control.

Gazanias are easy to propagate. Seed can be sown in spring, or cuttings taken in summer, but the plants layer themselves and you can detach rooted pieces at almost any time.

GERANIUM
Pelargonium

ABOVE: *The ivy-leaved geranium,* P. peltatum, *is by nature a trailer or ground-cover plant, which makes it a favourite flower for use in a windowbox.*

BELOW: *This magnificent display of geraniums would be unusual in cooler climates other than in a conservatory: but this shows what they can achieve given their favourite conditions – sun and a frost-free climate.*

There are four main types of these colourful old favourites: the zonal geraniums, the regal geraniums (usually simply called pelargoniums), the ivy-leaved geraniums and the scented-leaved types. They parted company from their cousins the cranesbills (see p. 35) nearly 200 years ago, but such is the conservatism of gardeners that we still call them geraniums.

The zonals (*P.* x *hortorum*) are shrubby perennials, usually making bushes about 30–40cm (12–16in) tall and wide covered from May to October with clusters of flowers in the white to red, orange, pink and magenta colour range. They take their name from the dark zone on the almost circular leaves: in some varieties this is elaborated into patterns of green, bronze, gold or white. First-class pot plants, they also make a splash of bright colour in the garden. In humid conditions you will need to watch for rust fungus: pick off and destroy affected leaves.

The regals (*P.* x *domesticum*) are bigger, to about 40–60cm (16–24in) tall, with much larger, ruffled flowers. They come in much the same range of colours, with the added attraction of darker, contrasting blotches on some of the petals, and have a similar flowering season, but have a tendency to straggliness – control this by trimming after flowering.

The ivy-leaved geraniums (*P. peltatum*) have red, magenta, pink, lilac or white flowers. A range of slightly weaker growers has the same colours marbled in white; a few have variegated foliage.

With less exciting flowers, but more interesting to the nose, are the various scented-leaved geraniums, such as the peppermint geranium (*P. tomentosum*), the rose geranium (*P. graveolens*) and the lemon geranium (*P. crispum*). Place a scented geranium leaf in the bottom of the tin when making a cake and it will suffuse its scent and flavour through the mix.

Because they are frost tender, the pelargoniums cannot be left in the garden and need to be overwintered in a greenhouse or conservatory, or they can be treated as annuals for summer bedding and containers. They need well-drained soil in full sun to grow and flower well. Deadhead them regularly to prolong flowering. When grown in warmer parts of the world they are evergreen, flowering almost continuously.

GLOBE ARTICHOKE
Cynara scolymus

The fat artichoke buds growing here with lavender and double opium poppies will soon open to a vivid blue. Mixing edibles and ornamentals in this way is an old cottage gardening tradition.

The globe artichoke is more familiar as a gourmet vegetable, but if you don't harvest the flower buds for the dinner table they will open out like giant thistles in a most unusual and beautiful shade of blue. Combined with the coarsely-cut grey foliage, the total effect is quite handsome enough for the flower garden. The flowers appear in summer on branched stems about 2m (6ft) tall. Try growing them with pink roses, or with other greyish-leaved plants such as bearded irises or lavender.

Globe artichokes can be grown from seed sown in spring and will flower in their second summer, but plants propagated from offsets taken in spring or late summer are faster.

Give globe artichokes sun and rich soil and allow each plant at least a square metre of space. They are quite drought resistant but they do appreciate being watered while they are building up their flower stems.

After the flowers fade, cut the stalks right down; the plants will then make fresh foliage which will last to be admired for the rest of the summer. After four or five years the plants will become crowded and should be divided. The best time to do this is in the spring.

If you allow the spent flowers to go to seed, they make wonderful material for dried flower arrangements. Waft some hairspray over them to prevent the seeds spreading and causing a nuisance.

HEARTLEAF BERGENIA
Bergenia cordifolia

This is 'Bressingham White', often considered the best of the white-flowered bergenias. As its flowers age, they turn pink. Other named varieties come in shades from pink to crimson and magenta; all have most handsome leaves.

Although its honey-scented flowers make a pleasing show in early spring, it is for its striking, almost circular leaves that the 'elephant ears' is most valuable in the garden. There are few plants that combine restrained growth and eye-catching effect like this one. The leaves grow from ground-hugging rhizomes and the whole plant, even in flower, is seldom more than 45cm (18in) tall. The plant is evergreen and in winter the leaves of the form 'Purpurea' take on most attractive purple tones – for the rest of the year they are deep green. The flowers of bergenias are usually mauve or clear pink, but deep pink and white varieties are available.

This is a plant for key positions: at a corner of a path, beside steps, where you want some solid underpinning to a planting of taller, flimsier flowers, or in a large handsome container. Bergenias will grow in sun or shade in any well-drained soil, but the best leaf colour is produced when they grow in full sun in poor soil.

Late autumn is the best planting time; the plants take their time about building up into clumps and can be left undisturbed for years. Don't starve them – some well-rotted manure at the end of winter will encourage lusher foliage and more flowers. Bergenias can be propagated by division in the autumn or the spring.

IRIS
Iris species and hybrids

ABOVE: The Algerian iris, Iris unguicularis, *would rank high in popularity in any garden and its habit of bearing violet-scented flowers from the end of autumn until spring makes it irresistible. Its only fault is that the flowers tend to hide among the abundant foliage, but this will not be so bad if the leaves are trimmed back in mid-autumn, before flowers appear. BELOW: This wonderful selection of graceful bearded irises shows only some of the range of colours available.*

Irises have been grown in cottage gardens since the earliest times. They generally have sword-shaped leaves, from grey-green to glossy green, and the flowers are typically arranged in multiples of three – three inner petals or standards, and three outer petals or falls. They are generally easy to cultivate and most will increase quite quickly. The irises are an enormous tribe, and just about every one of them is well worth growing; all we have room to do here is note a few favourites.

Bearded irises (*I.* x *germanica*) are well loved garden plants for the graceful carriage and wonderful range of colours displayed by their flowers in late spring and early summer. They are subtly and pleasingly fragrant too. They are available in just about every tone but true red, with many flowers featuring a beard (the tuft of hairs on the lower three petals) in a contrasting shade to the rest of the flower. These bearded irises flower mainly in June, though much shorter dwarf forms like 'Blue Denim' perform in May and open the season.

The beardless irises are usually scentless and mostly flower from early to midsummer. Chief among them, perhaps, are the glamorous Japanese irises bred from *I. kaempferi* and *I. laevigata*. The first thing you notice about them is the enormous size of the flowers – a bloom 15cm (6in) wide is not unusual – but they combine size with grace and beautiful colourings in the white, blue and purple range.

They grow to about 60–90cm (24–36in) tall and love rich soil, moisture and a sunny or semi-shaded site. The edge of a pond, where their crowns will be dry in winter but the roots can find their way down into the mud, will be heaven to them, but they do very well in an ordinary bed as long as they are watered generously from spring to the end of summer.

Bulbous *Iris reticulata* grows to only 10–15cm (4–6in) and can be used to bring colour and scent to the very front of the border in the late winter and early spring.

Divide irises every three or four years if the clumps become crowded. They don't like too much organic matter in the soil, but they do appreciate some artificial fertiliser in spring. Propagate by division of the rhizome or by offsets in late summer.

JAPANESE ANEMONE
Anemone x hybrida

Japanese anemones are as familiar as Michaelmas daisies and as loved. The common name is misleading: although naturalised in Japan, the plant is native to China.

With their graceful, cup-shaped, single or double flowers in white, pale pink or deep pink, the Japanese anemones bring a spring-like touch to the late summer and autumn garden.

That said, they are not the easiest plants to blend into a cottage garden. They are apt to look a little too classy for the annuals that have continued from the summer and, although they can be slow to become established, they spread rather extensively once they do, especially on sandy soils. This can make them unwelcome in amongst less robust plants.

Take a cue from their love of filtered shade and mass them amongst deciduous shrubs and trees, where their cool colours will be set off by the warm tones of the autumn leaves. Grow them with ferns and the like or try planting them as cover for spring bulbs so that you will gain two seasons of flower from the same spot.

Although many good named varieties do exist, 'Honorine Jobert' is still the most universally popular with its pure white single flowers with yellow stamens that appear for up to three months.

They will grow in any good garden soil in partial shade.

KAFFIR LILY
Schizostylis coccinea

Let your kaffir lilies star in a collection of late-blooming heathers, ornamental kale and variegated euonymus.

Standing apart from the abundance of plants that peak in spring and early summer, Kaffir lilies wait their turn until late summer and autumn when new blood can be a little thin on the ground. They should be welcomed into every garden for their red or pink flower spikes (almost like miniature gladioli) in October and November.

Schizostylis has a rhizomatous root system and is just as likely to be found alongside packets of bulbs as growing actively in the herbaceous section of nurseries and garden centres.

Kaffir lilies prefer moisture-retentive soil in sun, so dig in plenty of well-rotted garden compost or manure. They will quickly bulk up and may need dividing after a few years – spring being the ideal time. In cold areas, after cutting away yellowing foliage, it's worth spreading a layer of chipped bark or old fern fronds to provide insulation against penetrating frosts. The bright red variety *S. coccinea* 'Major' is frequently seen and admired. 'Mrs Hegarty' is a lovely clear pink. 'Tambara' is a softer red than 'Major'. Because of their tendency to flower well into November a sheltered site should be chosen, out of the worst of the wind and rain. All Kaffir lilies make excellent cut flowers.

LADY'S MANTLE
Alchemilla mollis

The lime-yellow flowers of lady's mantle here tumble over the edge of a path. They are borne in such abundance that the felted leaves can be completely hidden during flowering.

The name *Alchemilla* comes from the use of the lady's mantle by medieval alchemists who thought it would help them in making gold from lead; and you would think the plant was made of gold, so fashionable has it become.

It is a pretty thing, with its velvety leaves and frothy heads of lime-yellow flowers in summer. It makes an excellent contrast to deep-toned flowers. Dark foxgloves and some of the more purple-toned old-fashioned roses are favourites, and the 'black' varieties of bearded irises would be delightful, too.

The lady's mantle has rounded, pale green leaves with lobed and toothed edges that collect the dew or raindrops. The water thus collected was once reputed to have healing and magical powers. The plants form clumps about 30–45cm (12–18in) high and make good ground cover. It is widely used to edge borders and paths where the sprays of tiny, starry flowers will spill over to soften the edges of the planting.

Alchemilla will grow in any soil, in sun or partial shade. New plants can be propagated by seed, or by division in spring or autumn, although the lady's mantle will self-seed freely once established and can even become a pest.

LAMB'S EARS
Stachys byzantina

Stachys is a classic mixer, combining well with hundreds of plants, such as this blue-leaved lyme grass, Elymus arenarius.

As familiar as lavender, catmint and hollyhocks, lamb's ears is one of those easy-going cottage perennials that gets passed on by neighbours, for you will invariably find roots or larger layers if you draw back the dense furry carpet of grey leaves.

Stachys byzantina (*S. lanata*) is a classic 'front of border' perennial and a natural mixer with just about any shade of pink or blue. Used generously and repeated, for example in clumps down a border and spilling onto a path, it softens hard lines and colours which compete for your attention. Flower spikes of pale purple rise up to a height of about 45cm (18in) in July and August but it is for the velvet-textured leaves that stachys is most valuable. In fact, you may prefer the non-flowering version, 'Silver Carpet', or prefer to cut off the flower spikes to maintain the leaf quality. For something different look out for 'Primrose Heron'. The leaves are pale yellow, particularly early in the season.

Give lamb's ears sun or partial shade and good drainage and it will romp away. 'Silver Carpet' makes a fine ground cover to set off sedums like 'Autumn Joy' and 'Brilliant'. Less common but still worth considering are the betonies, *Stachys macrantha*, with whorls of lilac or pink blooms from May to July.

LENTEN ROSE
Helleborus orientalis

The Lenten roses bring welcome colour to the late winter and early spring border, and make impressive colonies, looking particularly well with the diminutive Cyclamen coum *and drifts of snowdrops.*

Hellebores are riding on the crest of a well-deserved wave of popularity, which is not surprising when you consider the qualities they lend to the winter garden. Perhaps the most reliable and eye-catching of all are forms of the Lenten rose. Unlike the more fickle white Christmas rose, Lenten roses settle down quickly in shady beds, borders or even containers and begin to form colonies by self-seeding. Perhaps their only vice is a tendency to hide away their beauty on stems which arch over. You need to turn up the flowers to reveal the attractive sepals, sometimes spotted crimson or maroon on white or green. Single colours include purple, white, slate grey, pink and pale green all with a prominent boss of yellow stems in the centre.

Flowering occurs between February and April, or earlier in a mild winter. When the stamens are shed, a fat beak-shaped seedpod begins to swell and if you want to save the seed catch them before they are shed (around July time). Sow them straight away in a seed tray and by the following autumn you will have plants big enough to return to the garden. After three years they will be of flowering size. You never quite know what's coming, but most are worth saving. You can also buy plants in bloom. 'Ashwood Hybrids' are particularly fine.

LUNGWORT
Pulmonaria

In addition to their display of spring flowers, many of the pulmonarias have leaves that are splashed with silver or white.

Lungworts are particularly valuable for providing one of the earliest flashes of blue in beds or borders in advance of all those bluebells, drumstick primroses and bugles. They are also tough colonists, able to cope with dry rooty soils under tree canopies. Some of the most eye-catching varieties are ones like 'Marjorie Fish' with white spotted leaves, more generously splashed than on the straight species *P. officinalis*.

Although 'Marjorie Fish' puts on a pleasing show of rose-coloured flowers, none of the spotted or silver leaved types produce such a vivid show of flowers as the plain green leaved varieties. *P. angustifolia azurea*, for example, makes a rich blue pool of blooms and looks stunning underneath pieris or with daffodils and doronicum. Reds are also well represented and 'Redstart' and 'Bowles' Red' will give a succession of blooms from February to April.

Clumps can be lifted and divided in the autumn. New plants are available in containers for planting throughout the year. Water them well to get them established and even established clumps will appreciate a thorough soak in drought conditions.

OBEDIENT PLANT
Physostegia virginiana

One of the best-known varieties of obedient plant is appropriately named 'Vivid'. The cheerful colours of the flowers and its ability to flower late when other perennials are flagging are its chief virtues.

The common name for this plant comes from a curious characteristic of the flowers, which are borne in short, snapdragon-like spikes in late summer: they are attached to the stem by a sort of hinged joint which allows you to rearrange them. This always delights small children, although these flowers are also pleasing to adults. These blooms may be pale or shocking pink, white or lavender. There is a form with neatly white-edged leaves, *Physostegia virginiana* 'Variegata'.

The plant spreads quite rapidly into a clump with each flower stem rising straight from the ground and reaching 90cm (36in), so it is very useful for giving a vertical accent to plantings of late summer annuals, most of which are rounded in habit. The obedient plant works well with white, blue or pale pink petunias, for instance, but avoid planting it with the red ones as the colours are apt to clash.

The obedient plant likes sun and and a fertile, well-drained soil. It is easy to grow, the only thing it asks is that you divide and replant it every couple of years – it tends to get overcrowded rather quickly. Autumn is the best time to do this.

PENSTEMON
Penstemon x *gloxinioides*

Bright and clear in colour, but never garish, penstemons combine especially well with roses. Both like the same rich soil. They are sometimes given the curious name 'beard tongue'.

Penstemons really look their best in a cottage garden, where the undistinguished foliage can be hidden by other plants. They bear their very decorative, bell-shaped flowers from midsummer through until the autumn if you keep the spent flower stems cut back. The flowers come in shades from white through pale pink and mauve to red and purple, many with white throats.

There are many good named varieties, but the seed is often offered simply by colour or in a mix of bright but subtle colours. Most grow about 60cm (24in) tall and, despite the Latin name *gloxinioides*, are hybrids of several North American species.

There are some very pretty, low-growing, smaller-flowered species from the United States too, that are suitable for rockeries or the front of the border. Perhaps the best known is the electric-blue *P. heterophyllus*.

Penstemons prefer full sun and a fertile, well-drained soil. Many of the taller border varieties are not fully hardy, although they may survive the winter in sheltered, well-drained conditions. As a general guide, the larger the leaves and flowers the more tender the variety. However, they are easily propagated from cuttings which can be overwintered under cover.

PEONY
Paeonia

Paeonia lactiflora 'Sarah Bernhardt' displays its huge, softly scented flower against beautiful cut foliage. The showy flowers are excellent for cutting.

The peony is one of those plants that found its way into old-time cottage gardens for medicinal uses and has stayed on in modern ones because of the beauty of its flowers.

Sometimes called peony roses, they do look rather like enormous roses and some have just a suggestion of rose scent. The colours are old rose colours – white through cool pinks to deep red – and the flowers can be poppy-like singles or have dozens of ruffled petals. They appear from late spring to midsummer, preceded by mahogany-tinted young foliage. The plants will die down for the winter.

Grow peonies in any moist but well-drained garden soil, in sun or partial shade. They are hardy, but flowers can be damaged by late spring frosts, and they will do best in a position sheltered from the early morning sun. Mulch the plants with well-rotted manure each spring, don't let them suffer too much drought in summer, and be patient – they can often take three or four years to settle in before they start flowering. Once they do, they are long-lasting and will still be there to delight your great-grandchildren.

PHLOX
Phlox paniculata and hybrids

The tall border phlox are happiest with a bit of shade. Creeping phlox can be grown in rockeries but the taller types look wonderful with other late-summer flowers such as daisies.

These showy perennials are good plants for the mixed border and make excellent cut flowers, as do the annual phloxes, *P. drummondii*. These easy summer annuals produce clusters of flowers in various shades of pink on small bushy plants from 15cm (6in) tall.

The tall late-summer flowering perennial phloxes, usually grouped under the banner of *P. paniculata*, grow from 45–120cm (18–48in) tall with splendid domed heads of flowers in shades from white through pink and mauve to red and violet.

Phlox plants are simple to grow, liking well-drained but moisture-retentive soil and preferring a lightly shaded position. They can be propagated by division in early spring or by root cuttings in winter.

The spring-flowering creeping phloxes, sometimes called moss pinks or alpine phlox, are usually classed as *P. subulata* and make mats of small evergreen leaves completely covered in season with dainty flowers in soft shades of pink or blue. They should be trimmed back after flowering to give a neat mat of leaves through the rest of the year. These are more suited to raised beds, dry stone walls or rockeries or to the very front of the border.

PINK
Dianthus plumarius

There are many varieties of pink, both named and unnamed, and all of them are lovely. It is an old cottage garden tradition to plant a row of pinks along the edge of a mixed planting, the ribbon of grey foliage tying all together.

Small cousins of the carnation, and predominantly in shades of pink, surprisingly the pinks do not take their name from the colour. 'Pinking' is a dressmaker's term for cutting fabric with a serrated edge to reduce fraying (using pinking shears): and the flower took its name from the serrated edges of its petals rather than its characteristic colour.

Not that pinks are only pink: they can be white or red, too, and some varieties are beautifully marked and 'laced' with maroon and crimson markings. All the pinks make tufts of greyish leaves, from which the 15–30cm (6–12in) tall stems rise to bear the sprays of flowers, and almost all of them are deliciously scented. The older varieties flowered in early summer, but many newer strains are repeat flowering, with two to three main flushes of flower throughout the summer.

They are easy to grow, and these evergreen, clump-forming plants like sun and well-drained soil. Keep the spent flowers trimmed off, both to encourage more flowers and to prolong the lives of the plants. They are not all that long lived and it is wise to renew your stock every four years or so by layering the plants in summer or taking cuttings of non-flowering shoots.

POLYANTHUS
Primula x *polyantha*

Polyanthus offer an endless range of colours, their variety further enhanced by the varying amount of gold at their centres. No two varieties are quite alike.

Few flowers offer all the primary colours in pure tones, but polyanthus is one. Yellow, pink, red, white or blue are all set off by gold stars in the centres of the flowers. The deep, velvety blues are especially beautiful, but all the colours are jewel-bright.

A hybrid of two English wild flowers, the primrose and the cowslip, the polyanthus come in two types: those that bear flowers individually on short stalks as primroses do, and those that carry them in bunches, cowslip-wise, on stems about 15cm (6in) tall.

There are modern strains with flowers up to 5cm (2in) wide, but the older, smaller types are by no means superseded. They include the gold-laced polyanthus: as well as gold stars in the centre, these have gold edges (lacings) to the petals, which are usually in dark shades of maroon and crimson, the better to show off the gold.

They do best in light shade and rich, leafy soil. All are suitable for container displays where they can be mixed with spring bulbs, pansies and forget-me-nots. Propagate from seed sown in early summer or divide clumps after flowering.

RED HOT POKER
Kniphofia

The old-fashioned flame-and-gold red hot pokers remain favourites. Most plants are hybrids. The species are seldom seen now but are worth growing, especially as several are becoming rare in their native South Africa.

The common name of the kniphofias comes from the tight bunches of flaming orange flowers that are borne on top of poker-straight stems, but in recent years the hybridists have succeeded in extending the colour range to pink, yellow and cream too. While the older varieties are massive plants with long grassy leaves and 1.5m (5ft) tall flower stems, many of the newer ones are daintier, with heights ranging from only 60cm (24in) upwards. Most of the red hot pokers are mid to late summer flowering.

When planting pokers, allow room for their foliage, which is grass-like and rather untidy. Agapanthus provide a splendid contrast in flower shape and colour, or you could build up a warm colour scheme with Californian poppies and yellow marguerites. They are all as drought-resistant as the pokers, which are long lived and as easy as can be to grow.

They will grow in just about any soil, and the only thing they are fussy about is sunshine: in shade they flower very sparsely. They can be propagated by division in spring.

The scientific name honours the German botanist Johann Hieronymus Kniphof and is pronounced 'niff-oaf-ear'.

ROSE CAMPION
Lychnis coronaria

Grey leaves and fairly small flowers prevent the rose campion seeming garish. This magenta version can be used to jazz up a planting of herbs; the white one looks good with more gently toned flowers.

The rose campion is one of those plants that survives in old gardens long after its owners have forgotten its name. It is rarely given a starring role, but it is a very good plant for filling in gaps – its grey leaves carpet the ground and the flowers are borne on 45–60cm (18–24in) tall stems for a long mid to late summer season. The usual variety is magenta-red, a much more subtle colour than it sounds, but there is a very pretty white version as well. Try them both with old-fashioned roses, with delphiniums, or even with some of the softer-toned daylilies.

Like most grey-leaved plants, the rose campion is resistant to drought and hot summers. Don't starve the plants, however: they will put on a much better show for some fertiliser and water. Cut the spent flower stems down and more will follow. Although the plants can be short-lived, they will self-seed freely if they are not deadheaded.

Other species of *Lychnis* are less often seen but worth seeking out. One of the best known is the dazzling scarlet Maltese cross, *L. chalcedonica*, which flowers rather briefly in early summer. It needs careful placement if the colour is not to shout down its neighbours.

SALVIA
Salvia

Spectacular when massed in a border planting, the spikes of Salvia x superba make a rich display of colour from mid to late summer.

The perennial salvias are much less aggressive than the red bedding salvias, at least in terms of colour. Most are hardy only in the mildest gardens, and some not even there. For example, the true-blue *S. uliginosa* will survive only the mildest winters in Britain. This is a beautiful plant for the back of a bed: it grows to 1.5m (5ft) tall, depending on how rich and moist the soil is, and flowers for many weeks in autumn.

The summer-flowering, 60cm (24in) tall *S. patens* matches *S. uliginosa* in purity of tone, although it is a much deeper blue. It rarely makes a mass of colour – just a few flowers at a time over many weeks.

S. microphylla syn. *S. grahamii* is shrubby in habit and performs a floral marathon from early summer to autumn. The flowers are warm and brilliant in colour but without being strident. Like all the tribe it likes sun and fertile, well-drained soil. It is perennial in mild areas. Trim the plant in early spring to keep it bushy.

S. nemorosa makes a neat, clump-forming perennial. There are also many good garden forms, such as 'East Friesland' ('Ostfriesland').

S N E E Z E W E E D
Helenium autumnale

The bold and richly coloured daisy-like flowers of heleniums are one of the mainstays of the late summer and early autumn border.

High summer signals the appearance of great clumps of yellow and mahogany daisies, flowering so freely as to almost conceal the foliage and with such a weight of bloom as to leave them almost bent double after rain if left unstaked. Flowering from July to September, heleniums will thrive in full sun and most soils save for waterlogged clay, but good ground preparation will pay dividends. Improve soils with well-rotted manure, garden compost or composted bark. Staking in late spring will also give the stray shoots time to envelop twiggy sticks or canes and loops of string so they are largely concealed. You will notice a falling-off in size and quality of bloom after two or three years. To maintain vigour, dig up and split the clumps, saving only the stronger pieces of root and stem on the outer edges. This can be done between November and April.

The colour range includes shades of yellow/orange and red, each daisy flower having a prominent central disc which, like rudbeckia, becomes more pronounced as the flower ages. They make excellent cut flowers, 'Moerheim Beauty', a bronze-red is the most widely grown. It reaches 90cm (36in) and makes a good companion for the yellow 'Butterpat'. 'Riverton Gem' is red and gold, 'Chipperfield Orange' taller than average at 135cm (54in).

S T O N E C R O P
Sedum

Use the white-flowered Sedum 'Stardust' to add a lighter touch to clumps of 'Autumn Joy'.

Challenging species or varieties are unlikely to make their mark on traditional cottage gardens. Ease of cultivation and propagation have undoubtedly helped sedums to become inextricably linked with a style of gardening in which a little neglect can add to the charm. Such is the diversity within this large genus that sedums could quite conceivably appear on walls, amongst rocks, in borders, in gravel, on cottage windowsills, even on roof tiles. Many have fleshy, water-storing stems and leaves, making them extremely drought-resistant.

Perhaps the most useful are the ice plants. Both *Sedum spectabile* and the taller 'Autumn Joy' ('Herbstfrunde') need no watering or feeding and reward the gardener with fresh clumps of flowers topped with flat heads and pink or salmon-pink flowers which act as magnets to butterflies in late summer (particularly *S. spectabile* 'Brilliant'). Even the spent flower spikes can add a modest beauty to borders in winter, especially when picked out by frost. Plant them near buddlejas and you are sure to lure in butterflies from far and wide. 'Stardust' is similar in leaf with white flowers while 'Ruby Glow' has trailing purple-grey leaves and ruby-red flowers. All can be bought in containers or propagated by splitting clumps or rooting cuttings.

S U N F L O W E R
Helianthus

'Loddon Gold' is the most familiar and readily available of the perennial sunflowers and is ideal to back up Michaelmas daisies.

Nothing cheers a garden as much as a few giant sunflowers with their heads in the clouds beaming down at you, but these are annuals. Perennial sunflowers cannot compete in terms of flower size, but win hands down when it comes to volume of flowers. They are all the more valuable for their appearance in late summer and autumn when annuals may be looking tired. Some species with running root systems can become invasive in small gardens and are best confined to wilder parts of the garden away from less robust types of perennials.

'Loddon Gold' is the most widely grown variety for sale, with double blooms on 1.5m (60in) stems. 'Capenoch Star' is an award-winning perennial sunflower with softer single lemon-yellow flowers on 1.2m (4ft) stems. Try it with the taller Michaelmas daisies like *Aster* x *frikartii* or 'Marie Ballard'.

If you can cope with its wandering ways you'll enjoy the vivid rich yellow pointed petals and black centre of *H. atrorubens* 'Monarch'. When grown next to the lawn, its suckering roots will be cropped by the mower. *H. salicifolius* is a common sight in gardens in the autumn with its narrow leaves and yellow daisies and at 1.8m (6ft) is of a similar stature.

STOKES' ASTER
Stokesia laevis

These unusually shaped, long-lasting flowers are a beautiful lavender blue. There is a chalk-white variety which looks well planted with the blue. Both will flower for many weeks if spent flower stems are removed.

This is one of the best fairly low-growing flowers for the front of a bed. Stokes' aster flowers from mid summer into the autumn, and the flat, cornflower-like flowers are a soft shade of blue that harmonises with just about anything.

These flowers may not be that popular in the pristine formal garden because of the constant need to deadhead the spent flowers, but for the cottage garden they are perfect. There is a white variety too, a soft, chalky white rather than a laundry-bright white, as well as pink and purple forms. All grow to about 30–45cm (12–18in).

The Stokes' aster (which is an American native, even though its name commemorates an English botanist) is easy to grow. Fully hardy, it will grow in sun or light shade. It has no fads about soil, but it is a bit sensitive to drought and is all the more lush for some fertiliser in spring. It can be propagated by division in spring.

Cut the spent flower stems down when the flowers fade to encourage more blooms – cutting flowers for indoor arrangements is an enjoyable way to deadhead perennials. And don't be too hasty to throw them out – the green involucres dry very prettily to a soft brown.

VALERIAN
Centranthus ruber

The red and white valerian are an exact match for size: the pink is a shade taller. All three are wonderful plants for dry summers, flowering for months on end. Give the plants a trim if they get straggly in mid-season.

Strictly speaking, this grand old-fashioned flower should be called the red valerian, to distinguish it from *Valeriana officinalis*, a herb formerly used in medicine but rather dowdy for the flower garden.

Centranthus ruber comes in pink and white as well as cerise red, the three colours looking very well when growing together. The individual flowers are tiny, but they are gathered together in decorative bunches and the plants produce them all through the summer. They grow about 60–90cm (2–3ft) tall, with light green foliage.

Thanks to its fleshy roots, this is a great survivor, enduring poor soil and drought that would have most flowers gasping. It is often seen in old country gardens and will even come up in the cracks in bitumen paving. Don't despise it for that – if you want a very easy-maintenance garden, this is one of the very best plants. All it needs is to be cut down at the end of its season to keep it tidy. With decent soil and some summer water, it becomes positively luxuriant. Try it with agapanthus and *Erigeron karvinskianus* – in some very posh gardens it has even been admitted into the company of old-fashioned roses. Propagate by seed in autumn or spring.

VIOLET
Viola odorata

Delicate and sweetly scented, violets are a traditional ground cover or edging plant in a cottage garden.

Violets lend old-fashioned, but enduringly popular ground cover to the cottage garden. They are well known for their perfume, but not all are scented. The one to grow for its famous fragrance is the sweet violet, *Viola odorata*, with its heart-shaped leaves and modest flowers. According to variety, these can be purple, a paler mauve usually catalogued as 'blue', pink or white.

The varieties vary in scent, but the purple 'Princess of Wales' and 'Royal Robe' are rewarding, and so is the pink violet, 'Coeur d'Alsace'. Sweetest and strongest of all is the rare, double white Parma violet, which comes in a pale blue version also.

All violets are low-growing, perennial plants that spread by runners and make good ground cover in shady places – but not too shady or flowering will be sparse. To enjoy the flowers at their best, you can trim the leaves back in winter so that they won't hide the flowers. Give them a moist, well-drained but moisture-retentive soil, keep them watered in summer and propagate them by detaching rooted runners at planting time. Violets also have a tendency to self-seed prolifically.

SHRUBS & TREES

with their mass and greenery make the most flattering background any garden can have. In addition to fruit trees, there are a wide variety that are appropriate for a cottage garden, whether you yearn for flowers, coloured leaves, berries, or decorative twigs and bark.

Use deciduous trees where summer shade but winter sun are called for, evergreens where you need to screen an undesirable view or to break the effect of the wind. The choice is yours, but remember when choosing trees that year-round comeliness is of more importance than fleeting displays of flowers or autumn leaves, lovely as these are, and you should select trees that will still be a suitable size for your garden when they are fully grown. As a rough rule of thumb, roots extend out about as far as the tree is tall, and so it is better to grow small trees unless you are planting a country estate.

Most trees will grow fast enough to make an impact in a short time if you give them a good start in life – plant them in good soil, generously prepared, and provide plenty of water and fertiliser during the growing season.

Shrubs serve many of the same purposes as trees, only on a smaller scale. They can screen views at eye level and provide a green backdrop and, being permanent plants, they can bring an air of solidity and permanence to a cottage garden, in contrast to the many here-today-and-gone-tomorrow annuals and herbaceous plants. There is an almost infinite variety of shrubs to choose from so we have had to confine our selection to just a few of those that you come across regularly in old-fashioned gardens. Among them you will find species ranging from those that grow less than knee-high to those that reach much more than head-high, and their uses are limited only by your imagination.

Like trees, shrubs are going to be with you for a long time, and they appreciate being planted into a well-prepared bed. Dig it well, remove any weeds, add as much organic matter as you can by way of well-rotted manure and compost, and mulch in spring and water in summer, at least for the first couple of years.

AZALEA
Rhododendron species

A Mollis (deciduous) azalea in full spring glory before its leaves appear. It will give splendid foliage colour in autumn. These azaleas have yellow undertones, with the whites tending to creamy and the pinks and reds to salmon.

Azaleas are old favourites, and there is no reason why a few choice specimens cannot grace the cottage garden, under a deciduous tree canopy perhaps, though it has to be admitted that the sort of mass planting that you see in parks and public gardens would have been way beyond the traditional cottage gardener's meagre budget.

That said, they are very attractive, shapely shrubs for lime-free soils and their foliage is good. The deciduous varieties give spectacular autumn fireworks before the leaves fall, while the evergreens are always neat and attractive.

Well-known types among the evergreens are the American Gable and Glenn Dale hybrids and the smaller Kurumes. These are slow growers, but they can eventually reach head-height and a spread that is rather wider than their height.

The deciduous azaleas specialise in the yellow-to-coral colour range. The evergreens are in the white-pink-red range, usually in cool tones, and the two don't really blend very well. But they match in their cultural requirements – light shade and a leafy, moist but well-drained soil, and they all grow beautifully in containers if you use an ericaceous (lime-free) potting mix.

CAMELLIA
Camellia

This spring-flowering camellia is a continuing delight to its owner. It is probably a cultivar of C. japonica, which was a great favourite in nineteenth-century gardens.

Camellias are most handsome shrubs, eventually becoming small trees, but they are slow growing and shapely at all stages of life, with notably handsome evergreen leaves. The flowers can be any shade from white to dark red, with some varieties featuring stripes and splashes of two or more shades. Flower shapes vary from single to double, with anemone, peony and rose forms. The old varieties are still available and as good as any, though the more recently raised Williamsii hybrids like 'Donation' are faster, freer growing and smothered in bloom. Most bloom during spring.

Camellias are fully to frost hardy, most varieties preferring a sheltered position in semi-shade. They grow well against a sheltered west- or north-facing wall (*not* east-facing) or in woodland, where they will gain protection from frost and early morning sun which can damage the flowers. Camellias also make excellent container plants.

Give camellias a good, lime-free soil enriched with leafmould, and avoid exposed or waterlogged conditions. Mulch each spring and trim to shape after flowering. Propagate by semi-ripe cuttings in summer or grafting in late winter or early spring.

FUCHSIA
Fuchsia

Single fuchsias are daintier but the ruffles of the doubles are hard to resist. Fuchsias are really delightful flowers for a warm, sunny spot, and for all types of containers.

As well as being one of the most desirable of pot plants, the fuchsia also takes its place among the favourite old-fashioned garden flowers. Hardy varieties are invaluable plants for the middle or back of the border, and can be left in place all year round, while the many half-hardy varieties can be planted out when conditions have warmed up in late spring or early summer. As well as planting them in borders as summer bedding, they are excellent container plants for pots, hanging baskets and windowboxes.

The original *F. magellanica* from South America has pendent red and purple flowers and grows almost head-high. It remains a fine plant, while its offspring can be single or double flowered, often with flared or elegantly recurved sepals, and come in seemingly every combination of white, pink, red or lilac. Some are upright in growth, others cascading. There are also several variegated forms. All bloom from early summer right through to autumn.

The faster-growing types are easily trained as standards, a form that shows off the hanging flowers very well. Half-hardy varieties can be kept from year to year if they are potted up and overwintered in the house or greenhouse.

BRIDAL WREATH
Spiraea 'Arguta'

The arching stems of bridal wreath are covered with white flowers and will look refreshing with Euphorbia characias *var.* wulfenii *and double yellow kerria.*

Also known as 'foam of May', this old favourite is one of a handful of deciduous shrubs whose modest beauty sits comfortably in a cottager's plot in a way that a tree magnolia or hardy palm could never do. Its arching stems are crammed with small, delicate white flowers on a shrub which, if left unpruned, can reach well above head height.

Given room to develop it can be left unpruned but may need lower shrubs to clothe the base which can become woody and bare. Thinning out the oldest, thickest wood after flowering will encourage younger wood to develop.

Other notable white spring-flowering spiraeas include *S.* x *cinerea* 'Grefsheim' which is of similar proportion to *S.* 'Arguta', and *S. thunbergii*, which is lower growing and earlier to bloom.

The summer-flowering spiraeas are largely red and pink and some have yellow leaves making them doubly valuable. *Spiraea* 'Goldflame' is truly a plant of many parts with copper and orange-tinted emerging leaves which mature to gold with an occasional variegated shoot topped with crimson flowers in July and August. 'Gold Mound' has clear yellow leaves and pink flowers and at 30cm (12in) tall is about a third the size of 'Goldflame'.

SHRUBBY CINQUEFOIL
Potentilla fruticosa

The summer flowers of the cinquefoils will mix very effectively with a range of blue-flowered shrubs like lavender, caryopteris and perovskia as well as hardy fuchsias.

You'd expect a native plant which occurs in cold upland parts of the country to both succeed well in our garden and sit comfortably in a traditional setting. Few other shrubs can match shrubby cinquefoil's floral marathon performed from May to October. In fact, this is the best way to consider them – as flowering plants – for the rest of the bush is pretty anonymous, with no great beauty in leaf or habit.

The range of flower colour has increased considerably in recent years to include tangerine, pink and red, though these colours do benefit from some shade during the hottest part of the day or the colours may fade. Some varieties like 'Goldfinger' have particularly large blooms.

Growth habit is also quite variable, ranging from the low spreading form of 'Manchu' through plants which make round bushes equal in height and spread, typified by deep yellow 'Knap Hill' and 'Red Robin' at 60 x 60cm (2 x 2ft), to varieties which grow taller and upright like 'Tilford Cream' with a height of 120cm (48in) and spread of 90cm (36in) after 10 years.

Pruning is not essential but reducing the spread by a third in spring will maintain vigour.

COTTON LAVENDER
Santolina

Grey-leaved santolinas look good grown in a border alongside purple or variegated sage, rue and catmint. Or try them in clay pots with scented-leaved pelargoniums.

The cotton lavender, with its aromatic grey foliage and yellow button flowers has a liking for sun and well-drained soil. Some gardeners prefer to sacrifice the flowers and prune santolina to within a few inches of the ground in April to give a tight mound of leaves.

The problem is that if santolina is allowed to go its own way and flower freely the foliage quality suffers and it can be split open by wind and snow. If you are aiming for a neat hedge around a herb garden or even an intricate pattern of interlocking hedges to form a lovers' knot, this pruning clearly makes sense, as does an occasional trim with shears.

The best form for hedging is *S. chamaecyparissus nana* which is naturally more dwarf and compact. Plant it at about 30–35cm (12–14in) apart. For a foliage specimen, *S. pinnata neapolitana* makes a dome of intensely silvery foliage with finely defined leaves, attractive throughout the year. *Santolina virens* is the only green-leaved species, still strongly perfumed but with lemon-yellow flowers which are perhaps the brightest of all and worth considering as a flowering shrub. Cuttings taken with a heel of older wood root easily in summer.

FIRETHORN
Pyracantha

The colourful berries of a firethorn will look good set against the yellow evergreen foliage of a conifer or elaeagnus or alongside a large-leaved variegated ivy such as 'Sulphur Heart'.

That romantic picture we conjure up of the classic cottage garden overflowing with hardy perennials like geraniums, campanulas and hollyhocks can become a bare wilderness of sticks in the winter without stalwarts like firethorn to add clothing, colour and, just as important, food and nest sites for the birds. Few shrubs are so adaptable, for pyracantha can be trained tight into walls and fences or stretched wires on posts, planted as a hedge, thorny barrier or windbreak or used as a specimen in an oak barrel to brighten areas of paving. However, it is worth bearing in mind that unpruned specimens are the ones that will bear the heaviest crops of luscious red, orange or yellow berries. It will grow well on every point of the compass and is not fussy about soil type. A clematis threading its way through a firethorn adds a lovely informal country flavour.

Select your firethorn according to its berry colour, vigour and habit. Young and more mature container grown plants are available throughout the year. 'Orange Glow' is an outstanding choice for wall training, the red-berried *Pyracantha rogersiana* will make 3m (10ft) all round after ten years left unpruned. 'Soleil d'Or' and 'Red Cushion' have a more spreading habit. In areas where fireblight is prevalent, choose any of the 'Saphyr' varieties.

HOLLY
Ilex aquifolium

When selecting hollies, pay no attention to cultivar names which suggest either male or female because often the reverse is the case. 'Golden Queen' is a male, 'Golden King' a female. (Both varieties are edged with yellow.)

Common holly needs no introduction though its true native haunts are in the Mediterranean which explains why in exceptionally hard winters holly can lose its leaves badly. There are some fascinating forms, some of which might be mistaken for a camellia and others which are so slow they resemble bonsai specimens.

The variegated varieties give the best value for money, especially if you possess a female which produces a regular crop of berries. This will depend on the presence of a male plant nearby to pollinate the female. Some female forms will produce enough male flowers to set a respectable crop of berries, so if limited to one variety, 'Pyramidalis' or 'J. C. van Tol', both green-leaved, red-berried forms, would be a sensible choice. For leaf colour, 'Golden van Tol' is a variegated self-fertile form.

'Lawsoniana' is amongst the most striking of the hollies, with irregular shades of green and yellow rather like an elaeagnus. Many varieties assume a pyramidal shape with typical height and spread of 1.8 x 1.2m (6 x 4ft) and 3 x 1.5m (10 x 5ft) for green leaved types. Holly makes a fine impenetrable hedge if planted at 45cm (18in) apart.

LILAC
Syringa

The twisted stems and flat-topped open crown of a mature lilac have an informal nature that make it a convincing choice for the cottage plot.

A lilac bush in full bloom is a joy; the whole bush covered in dense clusters of flowers that give off a distinctive soft, sweet and intense fragrance. The plant originally comes from Turkey, but most garden varieties were raised in France, such as the white 'Madame Lemoine', the pink and rose shaded 'Madame A Buchner', and 'Katherine Havemeyer', which has pink buds opening to lilac flowers. All are scented, but none so richly as the wild lilac, *Syringa vulgaris*, with its lovely lilac-blue flowers. The leaves, which fall in autumn, are, however, rather ordinary.

These handsome plants generally grow to 4–5m (12–15ft) tall and wide and bloom during late spring or early summer. Plant them in a sunny position in a fertile, well-drained, preferably alkaline soil. It is best to remove the flowerheads once they have finished their display, and to cut out weak shoots, especially from newly-planted lilacs to maintain the shape and encourage strong new growth.

Many lilacs are sold as grafted plants, so if an occasional sucker appears, remove it before it competes with the variety above.

LAVENDER
Lavandula

Those familiar with only blue lavender will be pleasantly surprised by this confection of blue, pink, and white cultivars, an ideal underplanting to roses.

The donkey-eared lavender, a form of French lavender, is well named with its elongated purple bracts, and it is intensely aromatic.

Lavender is a traditional herb and cottage garden plant, that offers its distinctive warm scent from both flowers and leaves, so it gives double value in a scented garden. An evergreen, bushy shrub with aromatic, narrow, grey-green leaves, it bears spikes of blue-mauve (or in some varieties pink or white) fragrant flowers for several weeks in summer.

There are many species and varieties of lavender to choose from, most of them are hardy but some are only half hardy, and the fragrance and herbal properties will vary with the different types. The heights vary from 30cm (12in) to 90cm (36in) or more.

There are several well-known varieties, the main ones being the English, French and Italian. The authorities all seem to disagree on their correct Latin names, but you can expect English lavender to be a tall grey-leaved bush with the flowers, lavender or white, in long spikes from mid to late summer. It is the largest and most hardy of the lavenders, most varieties reaching up to 1.2m (4ft). 'Hidcote' and 'Munstead' are popular dwarf forms, growing only about 45cm (18in) tall and wide.

French lavender sprawls a bit and is denser in growth, with shorter, fatter flower spikes and a slightly 'hotter' fragrance. Italian (or Corsican) lavender, the smallest of the three, has dark purple flower spikes crowned with a pair of magenta bracts. It comes in a white flowered version also. *Lavandula* x *allardii*, a hybrid between the English and French types, is good choice if you want plenty of flowers to dry.

All lavenders are best grown in an open sunny spot, but will tolerate some shade. They prefer well-drained soil, but it need not be rich, and don't worry overmuch about watering and feeding them once they are established – the fragrance is diluted if growth is too lush. The less hardy varieties will benefit from a winter mulch.

Trim lavender in spring and again after flowering to keep a compact shape and prevent the bush from becoming straggly. Do not cut back into old wood as this is unlikely to re-shoot.

Lavender has traditionally had many uses, including fragrant pot-pourris and perfumed sachets, skin and hair washes and a variety of medicinal uses, from treating headaches to healing burns, cuts and stings.

Both fresh and dried flowers and leaves can be used to flavour sugars, jellies, ice creams and cheeses. The flowers can also be crystallised and used as decoration on cakes.

MOCK ORANGE
Philadelphus

The young leaves of Philadelphus coronarius *'Aureus' are a delightful golden yellow in spring, and turn yellow-green in summer. Like most philadelphus, it bears fragrant flowers.*

The mock oranges are amongst the most easily-grown and free-flowering of shrubs, bearing their fragrant blooms in early to mid summer. Just about any ordinary, well-drained soil suits them and although they flower more freely in full sun they will also grow in part shade.

They are mostly rather tall, rapidly acheiving a height of 3m (10ft) or so, but their size varies a bit with the variety. They all have light green leaves that set off the whiteness of their flowers. Some are single (four petals) and others, like the much-admired 'Virginal', are semi-double or double. Most philadelphus are very sweetly scented, with a note of orange blossom in the fragrance, but some, such as the very beautiful *P. inodorus* var. *grandiflorus*, are, as the name suggests, almost scentless.

The usual varieties are deciduous and elegantly upright in habit. All mock oranges are suitable for cutting, and this is a good way to prune them, which it is advisable to do as they can become congested. Do a major prune just as the petals fall, clearing out some of the oldest growth, leaving unflowered branches to bloom next spring.

ROCK ROSE
Cistus

Rock rose flowers are short-lived, but the plants bear a long succession of blooms. This one is 'Brilliancy'. Grow them with other aromatic, drought-tolerant plants such as lavender, sage and dusty miller.

There are several species and hybrids of these Mediterranean shrubs, all well worth growing for their aromatic, dull green leaves, compact habit, and pretty, rose-like summer flowers. The flowers come in a range of old-rose colours, from white to magenta-pink, many of them having crimson blotches in the centre. The height of the plants varies from the 60cm (24in) of *C. salvifolius* to the 2m (7ft) or more of *C.* x *cyprius*, with the majority of varieties growing to around the metre mark.

Cistus ladanifer has white flowers with crimson blotches and outstandingly aromatic, sticky leaves, and is the source of the perfumed resin labdanum, which was used both medicinally and as an ingredient in incense in Biblical times. It is thought to have been the 'myrrh' presented to the infant Jesus by the wise men.

All are naturally bushy and compact and don't need pruning. Like many fast-growing shrubs they are not long lived and when they get straggly with age it is better to replace them from cuttings than to attempt rejuvenation by hard pruning. Cistus love sun, sharp drainage and a sheltered spot. All are outstandingly drought-resistant.

ROSEMARY
Rosmarinus officinalis

Rosemary flowers have a subtle scent, sweeter than the leaves. They are usually blue, but can also be pink or white, depending on the variety. It is a good herb to grow in containers, and also does well in coastal gardens.

Worth growing for its flowers alone, rosemary is also a gem to have near a path or doorway where you can brush against it or pluck a shoot to squeeze and savour as you pass by. It demands sun, shelter and good drainage. Older bushes can become woody and unresponsive to heavy pruning, so it is a good insurance to strike cuttings in the summer. Take these with a heel of older wood and grow them on to replace old, tired specimens.

On sunny days, cottagers would spread out the linen on sprawling bushes to take up the pungent aroma. Its culinary properties for flavouring meat, poultry and fish dishes are well known.

Mix rosemary in amongst other herbs. The golden sage 'Icterina' contrasts nicely with rosemary's blue flowers in April and May. On a sunny patio why not grow rosemary, lavender, lemon verbena, pineapple sage and eau de cologne mint in large clay pots?

In a sheltered garden rosemary can also be used as a clipped hedge planted at 60cm (24in) apart, for which the variety 'Miss Jessop's Upright' is the best form. A useful form for a lower hedge or a more manageable bush up to 90cm (36in), is 'Severn Sea'.

VIBURNUM
Viburnum

Viburnum x bodnantense 'Dawn' bears its rose pink flowers in mid winter. Use it as the centrepiece of a winter garden with skimmias, winter heathers and snowdrops.

Our gardens would be the poorer without viburnums for they are a wide-ranging and invaluable genus of winter-, spring- and summer-flowering shrubs. Some have a two-season performance in the shape of berries and vivid leaf colours. They are tough, robust and not fussy as to soil type. Picking six of the best from 200 or so is no easy task, but evergreen laurustinus (*V. tinus*) is such an established part of the winter scene with its white, pink-budded flowers that it's hard to leave out. Equally, *V.* x *bodnantense* 'Dawn' is a treasure, flowering on naked branches in the dead of winter, the blooms fragrant and frost-resistant. Later in April and May the richly perfumed flowerheads of *V. carlesii* are almost overpowering in their intensity. Sited near a door or window the scent will drift indoors. If space permits, the unique layered habit of *V. plicatum* 'Lanarth' is a real eye-catcher, the tops of the branches decorated with white lacecap blooms. The guelder rose, *V. opulus,* is a natural choice for mixed country-style hedgerows with flowers, berries and autumn colour, and 'Notcutt's Variety' is especially striking. Finally, *V. davidii* has a modest beauty in its dense mounds of dark green ribbed leaves. Female plants carry berries of an electrifying blue.

WEIGELA
Weigela florida

Use Weigela florida *in a background position where it can draw all eyes during its flowering but pass unnoticed thereafter. Or plant a coloured foliage variety such as 'Variegata', or 'Foliis Purpureis', which, as the name suggests, has purple foliage.*

'Florida' in this name has nothing to do with the state of Florida in the United States – it means 'flowery', a perfect description for this tall shrub from China. In its late spring and early summer season, it is covered with little bells, set off by the fresh new leaves. The blooms can be white, red, or some shade of pink according to the variety: one very popular type opens white and changes to deep pink as the flower ages.

Weigela florida is easy to grow – just give it a fertile soil and a sunny position – but the foliage is plain and the shrub is deciduous and not very prepossessing in its leafless state. *Weigela florida* 'Variegata' has creamy-yellow variegated foliage and gives a long season of beauty. After the spring flowers are over, the cream and green leaves remain eye-catching, although it looks best if most of the spent flower stems are promptly removed to encourage fresh growth.

The plant benefits from having the oldest, twiggiest branches cut right out every couple of years, and the best time to do this is directly after the plant has finished flowering. Like most spring-blooming shrubs, it flowers on the shoots it made the previous summer, and if you prune in winter you cut away the flowering wood.

WINTER JASMINE
Jasminum nudiflorum

The glorious mass of starry yellow blooms of the winter jasmine is a familiar sight in many a cottage garden. Although the open blooms can be spoilt by frost, it does not affect the buds, which soon produce more bright flowers to replace them.

If the familiar yellow winter jasmine was a great rarity, hard to propagate or a challenge to grow, we'd all be falling over each other to buy one. As luck would have it, *Jasminum nudiflorum* is bone hardy (although avoid easterly aspects as the rising sun will damage frosted blooms), it flowers for months between November and March, and will often form rooted layers in its eagerness to cover the ground.

Perhaps the winter jasmine suffers a little from a lack of scent in a family noted for perfume, and from the fact that it is not a true climber, preferring to spread its green shoots in a loose tangle of growth. Gardeners can turn this to their advantage by using it as a ground cover to tumble over a bank or wall.

When growing winter jasmine on a wall or fence, tie in the main framework of stems and allow young slender shoots to weep forward.

Their bright yellow flowers are particularly welcome, coming as they do in the drab days of winter. In April, cut back the strongest shoots that have flowered and cut back others close to the old wood to encourage a new crop to flower the following year. Ornamental quince makes a superb planting partner alongside, either wall trained or free standing.

WISTERIA
Wisteria sinensis & W. floribunda

Chinese wisteria can grow big enough to clothe a two-storey house with half a million flowers each spring. This is the old cultivar with lilac flowers. There is a white version too.

One of the best loved of all climbing plants, wisteria hangs its fragrant mauve or white flowers in clusters in early summer. There are two main species: the Chinese wisteria, *W. sinensis*, the first to bloom on its bare branches; and the Japanese wisteria, *W. floribunda*, flowering a couple of weeks later as the first new leaves unfold.

Both species are wonderful plants for a pergola, their delicate pinnate leaves substantial enough to cast good summer shade, then falling to let winter sun through bare branches. They are good for clothing the front of a house too. They do, however, need a strong trellis to twine on as the branches become large and heavy with age.

For all their vigour, wisterias are very amenable to pruning and training and you can hold the plants to almost any size you want – they can even be grown as free-standing shrubs. They will grow freely in almost any soil, and will thrive with the protection of a south- or west-facing wall. However, if there are small children about, it is wise to remove the seed pods as soon as they form for they are poisonous.

*R*OSES

You cannot claim to be a well-rounded gardener until you have walked in the evening amongst the nodding, cupped, pleated and quartered blooms that comprise the old-fashioned shrub roses. They ooze intoxicating perfumes and centuries of history.

Their season is all too brief (June and July) but inspiring none the less, and few plants can lay claim more persuasively to a special platform in the cottage border. However, with increasing demands on leisure time and shrinking plot size, few gardeners can devote the time or space to varieties that need training, pruning, and regular spraying to keep pests and diseases at bay. Picking out a few of the best would seem to be the answer and 'Charles de Mills' and 'Rosa Mundi' from the gallicas, 'Mme Isaac Pereire' from the bourbons and 'William Lobb' from the moss roses have loads of character and fruity scents. As luck would have it, modern breeders like David Austin have managed to transfer this charm and rich perfume and instil it in a new race of free-flowering, more compact and manageable roses. These 'English Roses' are now the height of fashion.

There are also some fine shrub roses like the rugosas that can be used behind perennials, as specimens or even in hedges and which will provide a succession of flowers and sometimes bright red hips too. The rugosas are particularly useful for gardens on exposed sites with poor soil.

Climbers and ramblers are indispensable for covering rustic timberwork, cottage walls and even trees. Mix them with clematis for a tapestry of flowers. Ground cover roses will also work well into the scheme of things in a way stiff hybrid tea roses never can do.

ROSES

ABOVE: Hybrid tea roses, 'Chicago Peace' (top) and 'Perfect Moment'. OPPOSITE (clockwise from top left): ● Rosa 'Leander' is a robust English rose that produces large sprays of quite small flowers in summer. The deep apricot blooms have a fruity fragrance. ● Red roses are amongst the most traditional of cottage garden flowers. ● This pretty white and yellow ground-cover rose is growing with white candy-tuft. ● 'Escapade', a bright pink, fragrant, cluster-flower rose. ● An old tea rose from 1894, *Rosa* 'Francis Dubreuil' bears crimson, almost double flowers. ● Pink-edged 'Ballerina' is one of the best of the continuous-blooming shrub roses. INSET: A pale pink climbing rose.

 If there is any single flower that belongs to the cottage garden it is the rose. Think of climbing and rambling roses wreathing your doors and windows; of shrub roses, either as accents in the flower garden or as informal, flowery hedges; of standards to bring that touch of formality; of bush roses planted on their own, among your summer flowers or even grown in the vegetable garden to provide fragrant petals and hips for pot-pourris and conserves.

Some people will argue that the most suitable roses are the old-fashioned roses, and they can certainly add a delightful period touch to the cottage garden. The nurseries that specialise in them offer a wide range of varieties of all types, and if you aren't familiar with them then a visit in midsummer when the roses have their main flowering period will be most rewarding. The only problem you might face is choosing your favourites, for these are the ones that have stood the test of time, and all are distinctive and beautiful.

There are some gardeners who feel that modern roses such as hybrid teas are not appropriate for the cottage garden, as their more rigid, formal shape and bright colours do not blend with the cottage garden style in the same way that the looser blooms and softer colours of the older varieties do.

There is, however, no need to turn your back on the modern varieties, many of which are outstandingly beautiful, but give priority to choosing those with fragrance – unlike most of the old roses, which are deliciously fragrant, many modern varieties have no fragrance, and why grow a scentless rose when you can have a scented one?

Look out, too, for the modern 'English Roses', which have been bred since the 1960s to combine the form and the fragrance of the old roses with the colour and repeat-flowering characteristics of the modern roses.

You also need to consider the variety's record of health when making your choice. Roses are subject to attack by various insects and fungus diseases, and it is no fun having to dose invalid plants with poisonous insecticides and fungicides. Their resistance varies a bit with soil and weather. Seek the advice of local rose lovers about which varieties are the best performers in your area.

It is often said that you should plant roses in beds of their own to make control of pests easier but they are just as healthy and easily looked after in mixed plantings, and they look better for low bushes of lavender, santolina or the like in front of them. The most important thing is not to crowd them: allow plenty of space between groups of roses.

Their requirements are simple enough. Give them at least a half day of sun and the richest possible soil, and water and feed regularly in summer. Pruning should usually be done in winter. Many old-fashioned roses, however, need little pruning; simply remove dead or diseased wood and overcrowded stems, and cut back as necessary to keep the bushes in shape. The exceptions for winter pruning are ramblers such as 'Albertine', that flower only once in early summer. They should be pruned immediately after they have finished flowering.

ABOVE LEFT: The blue daisy, also known as the blue marguerite, *Felicia amelloides*, makes a truly attractive small plant. There is also an elegant white-flowered cultivar and another with variegated leaves. ABOVE RIGHT: Shasta daisies are among the best of all cut flowers. They will bloom from summer to autumn if the spent flowers are cut down. The flowers can be single or double – the latter resemble white chrysanthemums. OPPOSITE (clockwise from top left): ● Rose-pink marguerites, *Argyranthemum frutescens*, bloom throughout summer. This is a tender perennial, but it is easily propagated from cuttings ● Marmalade daisies, which are also called gloriosa daisies, are an annual strain of *Rudbeckia hirta* (the perennial types are usually plain yellow). ● The pot marigold has long been a popular cottage garden plant, and comes in range of rich, warm colours. ● Everlasting daisies (*Helichrysum*) are usually grown for cutting but they are, indeed, just as worthwhile in the garden where they make a wonderfully bright show. INSET: A brilliant, perfectly formed everlasting daisy.

DAISIES

The daisy family is one of the biggest in the plant kingdom and one of the easiest to recognise. Everyone knows what a daisy looks like – it is what a child draws when asked to draw a flower. The botanist may point out that each 'petal' and each tuft of gold at the centre is a complete flower in itself so that the daisy flower is really a composite of many flowers, but the homely simplicity of the result and the fact that they are generally very easy to grow make the daisies indispensable to the cottage garden.

The daisy family offers both annuals and perennials in such wide variety of habit, sizes and colours that you could easily plant a flower garden with daisies alone. The only thing that would be lacking would be scent – very few daisies offer anything to the nose.

The annuals suitable for the cottage garden include the painted daisy (*Chrysanthemum carinatum*), the annual gaillardias and rudbeckias, coreopsis, argyranthemums, Australia's Swan River daisy and the everlasting daisy, South Africa's ursinias and arctotis, Mexico's zinnia, cosmos and tithonia, and, the king of all the daisies, the mighty sunflower.

All of these annual daisies are lovers of well-drained, fertile soil and they need plenty of sunshine.

Among the perennials there are such first-rate flowers as the gazanias, the seaside daisy (*Erigeron karvinskianus*), doronicums, heleniums and the showy osteospermums.

A small group are shrubby, including the marguerite, the grey-leaved *Euryops pectinatus* and the dainty blue daisy (*Felicia amelloides*), which although half-hardy is valued for its beautiful colour and long season. In autumn there are colourful asters and Michaelmas daisies. And, of course, we should not forget the ornamental varieties of the common daisy, *Bellis perennis*.

Most daisies are herbaceous plants, mainly flowering in summer and often of rather floppy habit – it is best to grow them in generous clumps for mutual support and to provide them with a stake. Most will stage a second flowering if you cut them back hard after the flowers are over. None of the daisy family is distinguished in leaf, and in the garden you will probably want to give them companions such as rosemary, lavender, irises and the like to mask this fault. All are good for cutting for indoor displays.

TOP LEFT: Rich blue hyacinths combine perfectly with the paler blue of violas in a spring bedding display. The flowers of hyacinths are richly perfumed, so plant them near the house or near a path, or grow them in containers and place them where you can enjoy their fragrance. TOP RIGHT: Yellow and blue is a classic combination of colours for a spring display. Here, the bright blue of muscari stands out well against a background of yellow daffodils growing along a cottage garden bank. There are varieties of narcissus that flower from early spring to early summer, so plant a selection for long-lasting colour. BELOW: White 'Monet' tulips mingle with bluebells, adding their cool charms beneath the spring blossom in this cherry walk.

$\mathcal{B}$ULBS

What would a spring garden be without the magnificence of bulbs? Even if winter hasn't been all that severe, the first bright days of spring are always welcome, and with them come the spring bulbs, the sunniest of flowers.

Bulbs push up from the soil with the first sign of longer, warmer days and before you know it what was bare earth only a couple of weeks before is covered in flowers. Not even the fastest of the annuals can match the miracle, and yet it has been a while in the making, for the bulbs have spent the winter making their roots and gathering energy for their big moment. Thus the gardener plants them in autumn, knowing better than to fret over the apparent lack of action.

You could almost advise gardeners to plant and forget about them, for bulbs are among the easiest of all plants to grow. The brown object you buy is a complete plant, flower and all, reduced to a compact package, and all you have to do to grow it is make a hole, put it in, and cover it up with soil. (The rule of thumb is to plant to twice the depth of the bulb.)

Chances are you won't even have to water your bulbs unless the autumn and winter are unusually dry.

It is after the flowers are over that you need to be more generous to the plant, giving it water and fertiliser to keep the foliage green as long as possible while the bulb is building up its reserves for the next year's performance. The problem is that the leaves are apt to get very shabby during the maturing and dying down process – and you can't remove them until they have died down naturally. In a cottage garden the solution is simplicity itself: you plant your bulbs among other plants that will mask the dying foliage. Later-flowering perennials are a good solution as they are rarely so leafy at bulb time that they hide the bulb flowers, and you can distract the eye with low, bushy plants such as lavender or rosemary, or plant annuals such as pansies that will sprawl over the bulb's territory.

Alternatively, bulbs like tulips can be treated like annuals for a seasonal display, then lifted and stored. This creates more work, but can be well worth the effort, allowing you to create a spectacular spring display, which can then be moved to make way for summer-flowering plants.

Of course, many bulbs also make lovely container plants, not only ideal for patios and courtyards, but also for placing in beds and borders, wherever you want to add instant colour or fill out a display. Once the flowers are over they can simply be moved to a less prominent position while the foliage dies back.

One point to note. In a mixed border, it's easy to forget just where your bulbs are after they have died down, and if you accidentally cut one in half with a spade you may well kill it. Always use a fork to dig where bulbs might be: a speared bulb is not a pretty sight. However, it will usually survive.

SUMMER BULBS

Bulbs are frequently associated with spring, but you could have a bulb in flower almost every day of the year if you wanted to. Many of the summer bulbs are perhaps less well known than the spring ones, partly because they flower when there is so much competition for the gardener's attention, but they include some real delights. Some will even continue into the autumn, such as the elegant *Nerine bowdenii*.

Foremost among the summer flowering bulbs are the many true lilies, most of which are wonderfully fragrant. Lilies have been a favourite plant in cottage gardens for centuries, and many of the traditional varieties are still grown.

Probably the oldest known is the Madonna lily, *Lilium candidum*. Once considered a symbol of the Virgin Mary, it has pure white trumpets with a delicious fragrance, strongest at twilight. Many other lilies are excellent for cottage gardens, including the more traditional martagon and regal lilies, as well as the many modern hybrids.

Whichever bulb you choose, however, it will offer only a fairly short season and, as was the case with the spring bulbs, you will also need to give your summer and autumn bloomers companions that will cover for them during the seasons when they are not performing.

You need to consider their foliage, too: unlike the spring bulbs, many are almost evergreen and can play their role in the summer palette of greens.

Like the spring bulbs, most summer bulbs grow happily in pots, which allows you to bring them forward – or even indoors – when they bloom. Repot them every couple of years.

ABOVE LEFT: The drooping bell-shaped flowerheads of the snakeshead fritillary, *Fritillaria meleagris*, have a distinctive chequerboard pattern. They are delightful in the informal setting of a cottage garden border, and will look well in uncut grass. White forms are also available, and a mixed planting is most effective. TOP RIGHT: Bright red and white tulips are set against the background of purple malcolmias. Tulips are also excellent as container plants. ABOVE RIGHT: Lilies and roses are a traditional combination for the cottage garden. Here the fragrant funnel-shaped flowers of *Lilium regale* mingle with the delicate pink flowers of *Rosa* 'Ballerina' in an English cottage garden.

TOP LEFT: In autumn the evergreen leaves of this holly tree almost vanish underneath the richly coloured leaves of the Virginia creeper that is climbing through and over it. TOP RIGHT: Pairs, or even threesomes, of interwoven climbers fit in perfectly with the free and easy spirit of cottage-style planting. Here, pink montana clematis shares space with honeysuckle. ABOVE: Most clematis have little to offer in winter, so the addition of ivy as a backdrop works well all year round.
OPPOSITE: Wisteria is a favourite among climbing plants for its grace and wonderful display in spring: all the species and garden varieties are very fragrant. *Wisteria sinensis* grows here with white marguerite daisies.
INSET: *Clematis montana* 'Rubens'.

CLIMBERS

 Just about every garden contains some eyesore – an ugly fence, shed, garage, water tank or what have you – that just cries out to be hidden behind a curtain of foliage. Climbing plants are the perfect solution: but you shouldn't think of them as being simply utilitarian. They combine grace and luxuriance in a way no other class of plant does, and many of them add lavish displays of flowers and wonderful scent as well.

They are well worth planting to adorn rather than conceal – to soften the lines of the house and blend them with the garden, to clothe pergolas, to decorate an arch over a front gate, to wreathe a tree in flowers, and many have the bonus of wonderful fragrance.

The gardener has an abundance of choice – beautiful roses, jasmines, passionflowers, honeysuckles and clematis in variety, and grapes, both fruiting and ornamental.

The many shapes and colours of the ivies add year-round foliage interest, and are especially valuable for shady areas, and the Virginia creeper will provide glorious autumn foliage colour.

As well as the perennial climbers, there are the fast-growing annual climbers that will cover walls, fences or arches with masses of colour. They are particularly useful for providing instant effect in a new garden before slower-growing plants have established.

Amongst the most widely grown are sweet peas, which have the added bonus of delightful fragrance, the cup and saucer vine, Chilean glory flower, black-eyed Susan, morning glory, nasturtiums, and, for rapid foliage cover, the gold-leaved or variegated hops.

Or, in true cottage garden style, you could use a vegetable, the runner bean, which makes an attractive climber in its own right.

Always, the first consideration is to match the plant to the space you want to cover. Certainly, you can discipline even the biggest growers but why make work for yourself?

Apart from ivy, Virginia creeper and a few other plants that can cling to a bare wall, climbers need to be given something onto which they can twine or attach their tendrils.

You can build a trellis, but often you can make do with a more discreet support. It can be sufficient to attach a few wires to your wall or fence, setting them maybe 25cm (10in) apart. They won't look pretty when new, but will be quite invisible once the climbers take hold.

FRUIT TREES

ABOVE: Although peaches will do best grown against a warm south- or west-facing wall, they can be grown in the open in sheltered sites. Or alternatively, why not grow one in a pot, keeping it outside during the summer, and bringing it into the shelter of a conservatory or greenhouse during the winter.

OPPOSITE (clockwise from top left): ● An old apple tree offers its summer bounty of fruit. In spring it would have been a mass of blossom that harmonised with the daffodils planted at its base. ● An ancient fig tree wreathed in pink *Clematis montana* spreads its branches over a deliciously formal small garden, with a terracotta birdbath framed in box bushes and daisies. ● A warm, sheltered cottage wall provides the perfect place to grow trained fruit. An edging of Sweet Williams provides a bright splash of colour and adds to the cottage garden effect. ● A plum tree covered in fragrant spring blossom — despite its appearance of antiquity it is only about thirty-five years old.

INSET: The blossoms of a Meyer lemon tree.

You may not want to revive the old cottager's habit of planting vegetables among your flowers, but the tradition of featuring fruit trees for their beauty as well as for their harvest is certainly worth continuing.

Naturally, you will want to choose the types that do best in your area. As well as apples, pears, cherries and plums, why not try growing the traditional medlars and mulberries? And in warm, sheltered places peaches, nectarines, apricots and figs can be grown too.

And there is no need to confine yourself to just those varieties that commercial growers find profitable. If you go to a specialist nursery you will find a very wide variety of fruits.

For the traditionalist, it is even possible to obtain many of the fruit trees that have been grown in cottage gardens for centuries, such as apples like 'D'Arcy Spice' from 1785 or 'Court Pendu Plat' from around 1200, or pears like 'Old Warden' that is known to have been grown since 1675.

Even in the smallest garden you can grow plenty of fruit by growing trained trees such as cordons, fans and espaliers against a wall or fence. And a sunny wall can give some of the more tender crops such as peaches the protection they require to succeed.

There is no need to hide your fruit trees away. They are every bit as decorative as trees grown purely for ornament; they are beautiful in spring blossom and colourful as the crops of fruit develop. As with all trees you need to consider how big they will grow, and to place them to best advantage, to frame the house, to block off undesirable views or make a backdrop to the garden.

Fans, cordons and espaliers can also be grown with post and wire supports to make a decorative screen, and the low-growing 'step-over' apples can be used to edge paths and borders.

It must be said that fruit trees do need more attention than purely ornamental trees. You are, after all, expecting a good deal more from them, and it makes sense to start with the best plants available and to plant them in sunny positions and the richest soil. There is no need to prune rigidly, but you will need to control any pests and diseases. Most trees need to be pollinated by another variety to give a good crop, so check their pollination requirements and grow compatible or self-fertile varieties.

HERBS

TOP: There are now decorative versions of many herbs, such as the gold variegated lemon balm (left) and purple fennel (right). ABOVE: Here the plain grey-leaved, purple-flowered sage plays its part in a composition of grey and soft green plants. OPPOSITE (clockwise from top left): ● Most herbs do love perfect drainage, and one way to ensure it is to raise their beds slightly above the adjacent paths – here heavy timbers lift the beds of dill, dyer's chamomile (*Anthemis*) and thyme by about 10cm (4in). ● This herb and vegetable garden, like most herb gardens, is a composition in greens and greys but its subtle colours can be very appealing. ● Borne in late spring, the rounded heads of purple chive flowers are first-rate for edging a bed, either in a herb garden or in an informal cottage garden. ● A small rosemary bush has here been trained as a standard, where it presides over a collection of brightly flowering spring flowers. INSET: Rosemary and rue.

A botanist will tell you that a herb is a plant that does not have permanent woody stems, and so it cannot be a tree or a shrub. Plants such as basil or thyme are clearly herbs, but by this definition sage and rosemary are not. They are shrubs! Never mind. Let us keep with the gardener's definition of a herb as a plant with fragrant leaves that can be added to food, or used for medicinal or craft purposes.

You don't have to be an enthusiastic cook to enjoy herbs in the garden. They can be grown for their fragrance alone, if that is your fancy. But anyone who has a kitchen will levy tribute from the herb patch, and so concentrate at first on those you like best to eat and then branch out into the less familiar varieties. And it is best to grow more than one of each so that you do not harvest the plant to death!

Classic favourites such as parsley, sage, rosemary, thyme and chives can be quite decorative in their own right, but many herbs are inclined to be a bit shapeless in their habit, and the traditional formal patch, maybe with a sundial or sculpture as centrepiece, does bring a bit of order to a planting.

However, there is no need to follow tradition. Distribute your herbs among your flowers if you prefer. Many are fairly low growing and look good at the front of the border, where their soft greenery will set off the flowers behind, while taller herbs such as fennel will add height and presence to the back of the border. Try planting herbs along the edges of paths, where they will release their fragrance as you brush past, or plant low-growing thymes and chamomiles amongst paving stones. They are resistant to trampling and will release their scent as you walk across them. And many herbs grow very well in pots so you can have the pleasure of fresh herbs anywhere. But remember to plant herbs for cooking close to the kitchen, where they can easily be reached without trampling across the border.

Apart from mint and bergamot, which revel in a damp spot, the general rule for herbs is well-drained soil, sun and not too much water or feeding – if the plants grow too lush, their scent and flavour will be less concentrated.

Some herbs are particularly fragrant additions to the garden. Of all the plants with scented leaves, eau-de-cologne mint has perhaps the freshest, most flower-like scent. The usual mint varieties are, of course, also worth growing. The variegated apple mint with leaves in mid-green and cream is the prettiest and least invasive. Bees love bergamot and it sometimes known as bee balm. The fragrance of bergamot leaves is a delight and the flowers are just about the brightest of any herb. Basil, too, is useful and the smell of its leaves is said to drive insects away, while any rosemary bush will add to the fragrant garden. There are so many to choose from; don't be afraid to experiment.

CREATING A FRAGRANT GARDEN

ABOVE LEFT: There is plenty of scent in this garden from lavender and the climbing roses; the daisies can be just eye-pleasing. ABOVE CENTRE: Plants with scented leaves are favourites for growing along paths, where you can brush against them as you pass by and release their fragrance. Here mounds of golden lemon thyme and grey lavender add tang to a kaleidoscope of early summer flowers. ABOVE RIGHT: Everyone loves the scent of roses but not all offer much to the nose. This one, 'Escapade', is pleasantly fragrant. The white flowers are candytuft. OPPOSITE: Cottage pinks and sweet Williams combine in an old galvanised tub to give a pot-pourri of fragrance. The edging is the dwarf form of golden feverfew. INSET: A hedge of fragrant lavender (*Lavandula dentata*) edges this path.

Of our five senses, the sense of smell is the least developed but that doesn't prevent it being perhaps the most subtle. Any woman knows that perfume is an important part of feeling her best. While a garden composed of scentless plants can be very beautiful, it is fragrance that makes it romantic and memorable. Many old-fashioned plants are delightfully scented, and no cottage garden would be complete without a selection of fragrant flowers and foliage, not only for enjoying as you walk through the garden or linger on a well-placed seat, but also for cutting for the house or preserving as pot-pourri or fragrant sachets so that you can enjoy their perfumes for longer.

The fragrance of a garden comes from many different things. There is the scent of freshly dug earth, heavy with fertility, the soft odour of new-mown grass and the sharp tang of compost – this is the smell of decay, certainly, but it is a decay that is rich with the promise of new life. After rain, the air in the garden smells fresh and sweet. These are the scents that signal that a garden is alive. It is against this background, which is almost unnoticed, that the gardener then weaves magic with the fragrance of flowers and scented leaves.

It is easy when drawing ideas from books to forget just how powerful this magic can be – scent cannot be photographed, and there are few words to describe it. We can say that a particular flower is pink, or blue, and the reader can then form a picture of what it might look like – but scents can't really be described except by comparison. You can say a flower has a scent like wine, but that doesn't really help much.

Plants don't give off their fragrance all the time in the same way. Night-scented flowers that may be overwhelming in the evening are apt to be odourless by day, and often the fragrance of a flower changes subtly as it develops. Many roses, for instance, offer a slightly different perfume when fully blown from that they gave when they were just opening.

ABOVE: A comfortable chair invites you to sit a little while and enjoy the blended scent of lilac and white banksian roses while they are at their early summer best. It can be moved when they are finished to wherever other scented blossoms are enjoying their flowering season.

OPPOSITE: Profuse and generous planting is a hallmark of cottage garden style. A colourful assortment of perennials mingle with annuals, bulbs and shrubs, while climbers cover the walls of the cottage. Many of the old-fashioned cottage garden plants are delightfully fragrant, so place these alongside paths and next to doors and windows so that you can enjoy their perfume whenever you pass by.

Scent varies with the weather, too. The scent of flowers is best on warm, humid days, and after a shower of rain. It blows away on a windy day, and evaporates rapidly if the air is too dry and hot. This leads us to the first rule for the creation of a fragrant garden – let it be sheltered.

As any garden designer faced with a client who dislikes pink (or yellow, or blue) knows, people's perception of colour varies greatly, and our perception of scent varies even more. What to one person is pleasing and refreshing, to another may be heavy and cloying. We know, too, that the sense of smell declines as you get older or if you are in the habit of smoking heavily.

Happily, the blending of scents isn't as fine a business as that of harmonising colour. Place two colours side by side, and the eye sees them separately, judging whether their juxtaposition is harmonious or not. Plant two scented plants together and, provided one doesn't overwhelm the other, the first impression you get will be a blend of the two. Move in closer and sniff each in turn, and the nose will forget the first one when sensing the second.

So, as long as the scented plants you choose please your senses, you can mix and match them without fear of clashing. But don't expect that anyone will notice the subtle scent of a bearded iris if there is a jasmine in full bloom nearby.

SITING FRAGRANT PLANTS

How should you place your fragrant plants? The real garden-scenters such as the jasmines and honeysuckles can be placed almost anywhere and the nose will seek them out. But most flowers offer their delights best on close sniffing, and you don't want to have to wade through a bed of other plants to reach them. They should be placed towards the front of the bed, lining the path where you walk, next to a favourite garden chair or by the front door where a visitor can enjoy their perfume while they are waiting for you to answer the bell.

Climbing plants with a strong fragrance are perfect for surrounding an arbour or garden seating area and for growing on walls next to doors and windows. They bring their flowers up to a height where you can most enjoy the perfume, and when the doors and windows are open the fragrance will waft into the house, so it can be enjoyed both indoors and out. Don't forget to include some fragrant flowers in your windowboxes and hanging baskets too, as they can be enjoyed in much the same way.

Scented leaves demand to be put where you will encounter them closely – most of them will not release their fragrance unless they are disturbed. Plant them where you will brush against them as you walk past: a lavender hedge along a path, a clump of eau-de-cologne mint at the front gate, or scented herbs lining the edges of vegetable beds, where you will brush against them as you lean over to gather cabbages. Low-growing, creeping thymes and chamomile can be planted between the paving stones in a path or patio. They are surprisingly tolerant of being walked on and will release a delightful fragrance as you walk across them. You could position a raised tub of aromatic foliage close to where you like to sit, or even construct an old-fashioned chamomile seat.

Flowers that only bloom late in the day or at night, such as the evening primrose and night-scented stocks, are well worth growing but need special thought when it comes to placing them. Most of us don't wander very far into the garden at night, and so they should be positioned where you can light them up and see them as well as smell them, such as by a patio or the path to the front door. The same applies to those that remain open but scentless by day, such as tobacco flowers.

With all this concentration on detail, don't forget the bigger picture. Fragrant or not, any garden needs to suit the way you live – you'll need trees for shade, carefully chosen to be the right shape and size for your particular garden and cunningly placed so that they allow in the winter sun; a place for the children to play; maybe a vegetable patch; and paths (of easy gradient, with steps as needed) to lead you from one part of the garden to the other – these provide the melody, the orchestra if you like, with which your scented plants will sing.

COTTAGE GARDEN CONTAINERS

OPPOSITE PAGE TOP LEFT: Crown imperials have the sort of quirky nature that makes them perfect for rambling cottage gardens. These yellow blooms have been underplanted with the ferny leaves and red pendant flowers of dicentra and the pot placed on a slab in a border to add instant height and colour.

TOP RIGHT: As an alternative to a windowbox, a large hay basket can be easier to fix, will give a larger volume of soil for bedding plants and it is easier to clothe the front edge too. Line the flat back of the basket with polythene to prevent the wall getting damp.

BOTTOM RIGHT: Sizeable clumps of London pride, house-leeks, variegated lemon balm and grey and purple-leaved *Sedum spathulifolium* 'Purpureum' make lively contrasts in shape and colour and will survive on a good soaking every two or three days. Stand them out on a wall or a sunny window ledge.

BOTTOM LEFT: Hardy annuals (pansies) and tender perennials (*Verbena* 'Sissinghurst') a half-hardy annual (*Salvia farinacea*) and cottage pinks combine to make a lively quartet that will give weeks of colour. You may need to insert some sticks and tie up the top-heavy pinks to stop them flopping down in the wind and rain.

Even if you can't aspire to the full cottage garden look, you can still sigh over a few cottage-style containers and dream of what might have been. To be sure of getting the authentic, slightly frayed effect, your pots and plants may have to dress down a bit for the occasion. Out go those classical urns, Versailles tubs and elaborate decorated terracotta pots, and in come the oak half barrels, simple hand-thrown earthenware pots, stone troughs, galvanised baths and dolly tubs.

Busy lizzies, cannas, begonias and space-age celosias must be shown short shift in favour of dwarf cornflowers, rudbeckias, violas, lavatera, morning glory and pot marigolds.

There are plenty of hardy perennials that can be mingled in to add a buffer to all

those flowers. Evergreen shrubs too, such as skimmia, variegated holly, *Viburnum tinus* and pyracantha can be included as specimens in individual pots or as a backbone to seasonal spring and summer bedding plants and are very valuable in winter. Informality is the key so avoid container plants that have been clipped rigidly into spires, lollipops or spirals. Light-hearted topiary, a fox, teddy bear, dove or fat hen will succeed however, whereas a row of clipped pyramid bay trees in classical style pots will be far too grand and ostentatious for the cottage plot.

Scaling up to trees, a small specimen grown in a roomy container like a half barrel can be invaluable to cast a little welcome shade on the patio on the hottest days and will provide a leafy canopy to soften house walls where a tree in the ground might not be practical. A variety of rowan like *Sorbus vilmorinii* will give flowers, berries and autumn tints. Snowy mespilus is also a strong contender with flowers and glorious oranges and reds at leaf fall. For winter flowers, the cherry *Prunus subhirtella* 'Autumnalis' would be a tempting choice, while for pretty white variegated foliage flushed pink when emerging, try *Acer negundo* 'Flamingo'.

LEFT: A wooden wheelbarrow has become something of a cliché when filled with trailing petunias and pelargoniums. However, lined with hay and filled with a collection of pots planted for seasonal colour it is easier to ring the changes. A late winter show like this can be wheeled under the house wall for extra protection.

PUTTING ON A SHOW

How you arrange your containers can add considerably to their impact. Clustered together on steps, window ledges, on the edge of wide paths and around doors and windows they will sit comfortably, especially if you bank them up and contrast shallow pans with long tom terracotta pots. You can mix plants similarly, putting the spreading with the tall and erect. Adding some *objets trouvés* around the base of your pots; fossils, flints, fir cones, driftwood, even rusty horseshoes, will add some rustic charm and reflect a little of your own personality.

Avoid rigid set pieces, two cabbage palms (*Cordyline*), for example, flanking a front door. It may be fine for a London town house but an asymmetrical style with perhaps a stone sink to the left balanced by a cluster of terracotta pots to the right will sit far more comfortably in a cottage garden.

Think also about using plants in pots to enhance and build on another eye-catcher in the garden. A sundial surrounded by pans of sun-loving thyme, sedum, chamomile and scented-leaved pelargoniums will have double the impact. Similarly a seat becomes immersed in perfume when you have stationed pots of tobacco plants, night-scented stock, heliotrope and mignonette alongside it.

BELOW: If you want to grow some of the most authentic cottage garden summer annuals you'll need to raise them from seed. The double dwarf sunflower 'Teddy Bear' is rarely seen for sale as a young plant but when combined with violas and pansies it more than justifies the extra work involved in raising it from seed yourself.

LEFT: Pansies and wallflowers will succeed together in almost any combination of colours. Line up your wallflowers behind the pansies in the autumn for troughs and windowboxes for a show like this in April and May. Scaling down the idea, use the dwarf wallflower 'Prince Mxd' with tiny violas. Pebbles are useful to cover bare soil.

TOP LEFT: If you've got plenty of space in borders then you can give Chinese lanterns (*Physalis*) their head and let them run around like mint, but containing the spreading roots in an old bucket concentrates the interest and prevents less robust plants from being swamped.

TOP RIGHT: Drawing inspiration from flowering borders, these terracotta pans fill a gap in June before summer bedding gets into its stride. Choose scented French lavender and Sweet Williams, each with a low drape of yellow-leaved Creeping Jenny and Lamium 'White Nancy'. The vibrant red flower is a selection from *Achillea* 'Summer Pastels'.

FOUR SEASON PROGRAMME

Maintaining interest in your cottage containers is more of a challenge in the winter months, especially before the earliest of the bulbs like snowdrops, dwarf iris and crocus burst onto the scene. You can always rely on winter heathers though and some, like varieties of *Erica* x *darleyensis,* begin to open in the new year, and the red buds of *Skimmia* 'Rubella' will look good for months alongside.

Dwarf bulbs will inject some colour later as will primroses and, amongst the perennials, lungwort, elephant ears (*Bergenia*) and lenten rose can be relied on whatever the weather.

As spring progresses, taller daffodils and tulips will add impact and can be used as high spots among those classic country style bedders – wallflowers, polyanthus, double daisies and pansies in mixed colours that rarely seem to clash. When there is still a chance of late frost rely on hardier summer bedders like marguerites, osteospermums and diascias amongst pansies and blowsy ranunculus. Hardy dicentras, lamiums and euphorbias will add to the appeal.

During the summer you are spoilt for choice but don't be tempted by highly bred, over-sophisticated types as these reduce to mere blobs of colour at ankle height. With regular watering, feeding and deadheading many will carry on until the frosts. There are lots of ideas on these pages to show you how to pick and mix and create a memorable show.

Finally, seek out the best colour mixtures. 'Antique' pansies and annual Phlox 'Tapestry' are delectable while *Brachyscome* 'Bravo' soothes many a colour clash. With so much choice and an almost endless list of combinations, the danger is you'll run out of space all too soon!

OPPOSITE: Bring your cottage garden indoors by picking a variety of flowers such as these. Roses, daisies, tulips, cornflowers, irises and heads of viburnum are here combined into a colourful cottage-style arrangement.

CUT FLOWERS

 Gardens full of flowers are a major delight, but we spend much of our time indoors, away from their beauty. Potted plants in bloom can be brought inside, or you can use vases of cut flowers to create a garden-like atmosphere in any room.

PICKING FLOWERS

Always pick flowers from the garden in the cool of the day, early in the morning or late in the afternoon, and put them in a cool place for a couple of hours to recover. (If you're picking a bunch of flowers from your garden for a friend, give them at least half an hour in water before tying them up.)

ARRANGING FLOWERS

Before arranging the flowers, cut a few centimetres off the stems, under water, with sharp secateurs. Don't crush the stems; cut them off cleanly so that they can take up water easily. Strip off any leaves that are likely to be under the water, as they will rot rapidly, polluting the water and giving off a rotting smell.

Be sure your vases and the water are perfectly clean; if necessary, wash the vases out with bleach to remove old stains. Change the water daily and top it up as necessary. You may use a purchased floral preservative, or make your own by adding sugar and bleach to the water.

On page 79 you will find details of some popular flowers suitable for cutting.

REVIVING FLOWERS

If flowers start to droop, it is often because an air lock has formed in the stem. The easiest way to revive them is to cut 2–3cm (1in) off the stem and place the flowers upright in water with the water reaching up to the head. Let them stand for several hours. This is the best treatment for most bulb flowers – tulips, daffodils, lilies, irises. Another way of reviving wilting flowers is to stand them in a couple of centimetres of boiling water. When the water is cool, they should have revived. Then recut the stems under water, removing the boiled bits of stem, and give the flowers an hour or two in deep water.

PLACING ARRANGEMENTS

Place your arrangements out of direct sunlight and draughts, and away from fruit because the ethylene given off by ripening fruit will age the flowers rapidly.

BUYING FLOWERS

If you wish to supplement your own garden flowers, choose ones that are bright and fresh looking and just starting to open. Avoid those with yellow leaves or slimy, brown stems that have obviously been sitting around for some time. And remember that flowers exposed to sunlight or strong winds will age faster. When you get home, put them into cold water immediately.

SPECIAL HINTS

Re-cut the stems of woody stemmed flowers, such as **rhododendrons**, **lilacs**, **azaleas** and **magnolias**, under water, taking off a centimetre or so, and remove all excess foliage. Some people like to split the ends of the stem for about a centimetre.

Roses are delicate and they should be cut during the cool of the day, re-cutting their stems under water. They don't like the water too cold and must be kept out of the sun. Remove all thorns to make them easier to handle – this also creates extra places where the stems can absorb water. Don't cut too many flowers on long stems or you risk weakening the bush; and in any case you will find that short-stemmed roses will last longer.

Flowers with sticky sap, such as **dahlias**, **cosmos** and **poppies**, need their cut stems cauterised or they will bleed to death. Either plunge them into a centimetre or two of boiling water for a minute or so, or pass the ends through a flame for a few seconds.

Daffodils and **hyacinths** are an exception: they like to have their excess sap gently squeezed out.

Poppies are best if the water in the vase is only a few centimetres deep – the stems are apt to rot in deep water.

Stocks and **wallflowers** foul their water very quickly and so they look awful in glass vases. Be extra careful to remove any leaves that will be under water and be sure to change the water regularly.

The leaves of **chrysanthemums** die off faster than the flowers. When the leaves become tatty, strip them all and then rearrange the flowers.

Camellias absorb water faster through their faces than the stems and they last best if you spray them daily. Handle them with care because they bruise easily.

Violets absorb water similarly – the best method with them is to dunk the whole bunch in water daily.

Each **hibiscus** flower will live only a day, dying in the evening, but you can usually keep them fresh through a dinner party if you cut them in the morning and store them in the fridge until the last moment.

PLANTS FOR CUTTING

When you've got your flowering borders up and running another urge is almost certain to take hold; the desire to decorate your porch, hall, windowsills, mantelpiece and even dressing table with blooms that encapsulate the very essence of the cottage garden style. Don't be surprised that by placing flowers in such close proximity to each other a whole stream of planting ideas present themselves. In addition, the scent from blooms confined indoors will, of course, be far less elusive than in the garden, especially on breezy days.

Both the containers for your cut flowers and the flowers themselves should suggest a breath of country air. The cottage garden style has certainly been influential in the trend towards a much more relaxed and spontaneous approach to arranging flowers. Stiff and formal, triangular and 'L'-shaped designs are far too contrived for the cottage window. Even when embellished with grapes and gold cherubs they have invisible lines dictating the boundaries. The secret is to make your cut flowers look as though they haven't been 'arranged' at all – though a motley selection of plants merely stuffed into a jam jar with foliage submerged under the water will neither look the part nor last long.

One of the nicest aspects of cut flower cottage garden style is that you are harvesting the fruits of your own labour. They will fit in perfectly with their environment,

blurring the dividing line between home and garden, whether glimpsed from a pathway, through an open window or framing a view from your favourite armchair. During cold spells in winter and spring, what could be more delightful than the scent from winter iris or more delicate than a small bouquet of snowdrops with the gossamer-like seed heads of old man's beard?

Planting up a selection of shrubs, perennials and bulbs that will link together to form a continuous stream of flower production for twelve months of the year is one secret of success. For foliage, variegated forms of euonymus, weigela and elaeagnus are invaluable.

TOP LEFT: Posies of primroses and grape hyacinths, dwarf daffodils and drumstick primulas will bring a breath of spring to your home.

TOP RIGHT: Pansies, love-in-a-mist, cosmos and pot marigolds will seed themselves each year. Add Michaelmas daisies, single annual asters and chrysanthemums for a real late summer festival of colour.

BELOW: Teapots filled with asters, pansies, fuchsias and nasturtiums arranged on a tray of autumn leaves and ripe crab apples makes an eye-catching table decoration.

FLOWER CRAFTS

 Bringing flowers indoors can increase the pleasure you get from your garden, but, unfortunately, cut flowers die quickly. Flower crafts – that is, those crafts that use fresh or, more often, dried flowers to add beauty and fragrance to your life – allow you to extend the usefulness of the flowers for a much longer period of time. Most crafts use dried flowers as the drying process prolongs their beauty and fragrance.

Bunches of dried flowers can look lovely in themselves, or the flowers can be more formally arranged in wreaths and wall hangings. Petals, sprigs and leaves can be made into pot-pourris that will be used to perfume the house, or they can be packaged into sachets or little fragrant pillows. Tuck them away to scent drawers and cupboards, storage areas or bags, or tie them to door knobs or chair backs for a decorative effect.

Roses and lavender are among the most popular flowers for drying as they retain their fragrance and shape well. Many of the herbs such as rosemary, lemon verbena, oregano and thyme are useful additions.

Flowers and herbs can also be used to make perfumed waters and oils and a variety of cosmetic products, such as face cleansers, skin fresheners, moisturisers and hair rinses. Packaged in attractive bottles and decorated with ribbon, they also make attractive gifts.

You can also press flowers and use them as pictures and to decorate any number of things, from pictures and bookmarks to cards and candles.

There are few joys in life that surpass that of making something. All craftspeople know this, but they also know how disappointing it can be if the idea fails, especially if a lot of effort has been put in. The simple projects described here have been chosen so that they can be made by everyone – try them and you too will have created something beautiful.

DRYING FLOWERS

Drying flowers for use in wreaths, hangings and pot-pourris has become increasingly popular. With only a little effort you can preserve their colour and fragrance for future pleasure.

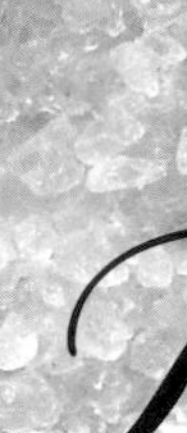

There are several ways to dry flowers, depending on the type of flower and the way you want to use it. Some methods preserve the shape of the flower better than others; some are practical only for petals or foliage. Investigate the different methods before selecting one for your flowers. The simplest of the processes is air drying and it has the added advantage that the bunches of flowers, hanging from racks, poles or the ceiling, look decorative while they are drying. Other drying processes include the silica gel, glycerine and microwave techniques.

Freeze drying is a commercial technique in which flowers are preserved by freezing the moisture in stems and blooms and then removing it, while retaining the shape and original colour of the material. Freeze-dried flowers are available from dried flower outlets and florists' shops.

SILICA GEL DRYING

Silica gel drying is best for flowers with delicate petals such as daisies, roses and pansies, and can be purchased from craft shops. The amount you need will depend on the size of the container and the number of flowers you want to dry at any one time. Always buy the blue crystals because they turn pink when moisture has been absorbed. If that happens, place them in a shallow tray inside an oven heated to 130°C to dry out (the colour will return to blue).

If only the flowers are to be dried, follow the steps on the opposite page, and use a shallow plastic container.

Silica gel is ideal for drying flowers with delicate petals that might be damaged with most other drying methods. Shown here (clockwise from the top left) are pinks, Dutch iris, double narcissus, larkspurs, rosebuds, calendulas, lilac, tulips and love-in-a-mist. As the silica gel absorbs moisture from the petals (and the air) it will turn from blue to pink, as it has here. It can then be dried out in the oven and will be ready to be used again.

Step 1 Place silica gel in a container until it is 1.25–2.5cm (0.5–1in) deep, and then place the heads of the flowers on top of the crystals, making sure the petals do not overlap.

Step 2 Spoon more crystals under, between and finally over the flowers until they are completely covered, taking care that the petals are not damaged. After two or three days, check to see the flowers have dried, and then pour off the crystals. Use a fine paintbrush to clean any crystals from the flowers.

To dry whole flowers, including the stems, make a shelf from foil-covered cardboard to fit inside a deep container. At even intervals in the shelf pierce holes (very slightly larger than the diameter of the stems) and thread the stems through the shelf, so that the flower heads sit flat on top of the shelf and the stems hang down. Also leave holes in the shelf to pour in silica gel. Fill the container with crystals, making sure they are under, between and around the flowers, and then seal it and leave the flowers to dry in the same way as before.

MICROWAVE DRYING

There are no definite rules for microwaving flowers and much of the process is trial and error. It is best to use less mature foliage, or the flowers and leaves may fall off after microwaving. As with all drying methods, always pick flowers and foliage when they are dry, never after rain or before dew has evaporated.

Foliage is best dried by placing the leaves in a paper bag, which is then folded over at the end and placed on top of a microwave-proof bowl, or by placing them between layers of absorbent paper. Microwave them on MEDIUM for about 2 minutes, then check. It will take 2–5 minutes, depending on the type of foliage. Microwave in short bursts until the desired effect is achieved.

Flowers dry best in the microwave when placed in a microwave-proof dish with silica gel. Cover the base of the dish with about 5cm (2in) of crystals and rest the flowerheads on top, poking any short stems into the crystals. Cover with more crystals and place the dish in the oven with half a cup of water in another container. Cook on MEDIUM for 2–4 minutes, checking progress during the cooking. Let flowers with delicate petals stand for at least 10 minutes after microwaving and those with large petals for 30 minutes.

AIR DRYING

Air drying is the simplest and most commonly used technique for drying flowers, since very little equipment is needed and the technique is suitable for almost all flowers. Only heavy-headed or very delicate flowers, such as spring blooms, are unsuitable.

Pick flowers for drying as early in the day as possible so that they are quite fresh. Remove excess foliage and gather the flowers into bunches. Fasten the bunches together firmly using an elastic band, and then thread florists' wire through and around the stems of the flowers, leaving a long length of wire at the end from which to hang up the bunch.

Hang the bunches upside down in a dry and airy place, leaving enough space for the air to circulate between them. Try to hang them out of direct sunlight. Always put your flowers in the place where they will dry most quickly as this will give the best results and ensure that they do not become mouldy.

The flowers can be hung from a laundry rack or from bamboo poles or branches suspended from the ceiling. In this way the flowers dry efficiently while providing a colourful display.

It will take anything from five days to three weeks for the flowers to dry, depending on the type of blooms and the weather. When completely dry the flowers should feel slightly crisp and the leaves should be dry and brittle.

Flowers with woody stems can be dried standing upright in a container but they will need to be supported. Place chicken wire over the top of the container and thread the stems through to prevent them from becoming damaged. Petals for pot-pourris or sachets can be dried spread on a wire rack or newspaper.

GLYCERINE DRYING

Glycerine, used for drying foliage, can be purchased from pharmacies or craft shops. Mix one part glycerine with two of boiling water, stir and pour into a jug.

Cut the stems of the foliage on an angle under warm water, and stand them in the solution (the stems should be covered with 10–15cm (4–6in) of the solution). Place the container in a cool, dry, dark place until the leaves have absorbed the mixture and changed colour. The drying time will be 2–3 weeks; check every so often to see if the solution needs topping up. When the stems are ready, remove them and wash them in clean water. Then dry them on blotting paper.

ABOVE: Air drying is the simplest way to dry flowers and seedheads and is suitable for many. Here are (left to right) larkspurs, wheat, roses, lavender, marguerites and yellow calendulas. The bunches have a cottagey feel as they dry.

ℬATH BAGS

Nothing is more relaxing than settling back in a warm bath

scented with herbs and floral notes. Just tie a bath bag to the tap

and run the water over it to release the fragrance.

 These bath sachets are made from muslin and can be tied up with raffia, string or hessian ribbon, which can in turn be tied onto the bath tap. The water runs over the bag, perfuming the bath. Bath bags can be quite small, about 10cm (4in) long and 5cm (2in) wide.

The herbal bags can be reused for several baths; the oatmeal recipe will leave the skin feeling soft and refreshed but can be used only once. The mixtures should be prepared following the instructions for making pot-pourri for a sachet (page 88).

ABOVE LEFT: Muslin bath bags tied with string make perfect gifts. Make six or eight and pack them in a small box for the best effect. Choose a lovely colourful box and pretty ribbons or continue the natural, cottagey look with a cardboard box and raffia.

Soothing herbal bath bags

½ cup lavender
½ cup mint or peppermint
½ cup rose petals
½ cup chamomile

Skin softening bath bag

1 cup oatmeal
1 cup mixed herbs such as
    rosemary, lemon verbena
    sage or bay leaf

POT-POURRIS

Beautifully scented, colourful pot-pourris of dried leaves and flowers have long been used to bring fragrances from the garden into the house.

 Pot-pourris can be made from any of the scented flowers or herbs in the garden. Experiment to find a mix you like, or make up any one of the lovely recipes on these pages. Your pot-pourri can be displayed in a pretty ceramic bowl or in any of your favourite containers.

MATERIALS

DRIED MATERIAL
Always use the best quality dried material in your pot-pourri as it has to be visually pleasing as well as fragrant. Choose flowerheads in full bloom and add herbs, nuts, berries, cinnamon sticks, pine needles and citrus peels.

FIXATIVES
The dried ingredients are the base of a pot-pourri but a fixative is needed to make sure that the fragrance will be lasting. A number of different fixatives are available from herbal suppliers, shops selling natural beauty and health products, and some pharmacies and craft shops. The most commonly used is orris root powder but it must be used sparingly or the pot-pourri will have a dusty look. Other fixatives include oakmoss, gum benzoin, cloves and spices, and tonka beans.

ESSENTIAL OILS
The final ingredient in a pot-pourri is a scented oil. The amount of oil added to a pot-pourri will vary according to the quantity of dried materials and can be increased to suit personal taste. The oils help to keep the mixture fragrant and additional oil can be added whenever necessary to replenish the fragrance of an old pot-pourri.

Spicy Lemon and Lavender Pot-pourri

2 cups lavender
1 cup lemon verbena
1/2 cup lemon-scented geranium leaves
1/4 cup crushed cinnamon sticks
1/4 cup dried lemon peel
2 tbsp whole cloves
1 tbsp crushed cloves
2 teaspoons allspice
1 teaspoon nutmeg
1 tablespoon orris root powder
10 drops lavender oil
5 drops lemon verbena oil

**Old-fashioned Rose
Pot-pourri**

3 cups mixed rose petals

½ cup lemon verbena

1 tablespoon orris root
   powder

¼ cup oakmoss, chopped
   into small pieces

10–15 drops rose oil

**Mixed Floral and Herb
Pot-pourri**

1 cup rose petals

½ cup lavender

¼ cup violets

¼ cup cornflowers

½ cup marigold flowers

½ cup sweet mixed herbs

1 tablespoon orris root
   powder

2 teaspoons cinnamon
   powder

5 drops rose oil

3 drops lavender oil

2 drops lemon oil

Cottage Garden Pot-pourri

4 cups rose petals

2 cups rose geranium leaves

2 cups flowers such as freesias, jasmine, delphiniums

½ cup eau-de-cologne mint

½ cup marjoram

½ cup lemon verbena

6 sticks cinnamon

¼ cup cloves, coarsely ground

1 cup oakmoss

Few drops rose oil

Few drops geranium oil

Pressed pansies

MAKING A DRY POT-POURRI

MATERIALS

Dried material • Fixatives • Essential oil • Measuring cups • Glass eyedroppper • Mixing bowls • Scoop • Wooden spoons • Clothes pegs • Brown paper bags

Step 1 Place all the dried materials in a mixing bowl and gently mix them together with a wooden spoon, being careful not to break the flower petals.

Step 2 Place the spices and fixatives in another mixing bowl and, using the eyedropper, add the essential oil. (Remember, extra oil can be added later if the scent is not strong enough.) Mix these ingredients together thoroughly.

Step 3 Add the fixative and oil mixture to the dried materials and stir with a wooden spoon. Place the mixture in a brown paper bag that is large enough for the mixture to be shaken inside. Fold the end over and hold it closed with a clothes peg. (An extra bag can be used as a lining if the mixture is quite oily.)

Step 4 Store the mixture in a cool, dark place for 2–4 weeks, shaking the bag gently every 2–3 days to blend the ingredients. When the pot-pourri is ready, scoop it out, place the mixture in a container and decorate the top with extra dried flowerheads, if desired.

BELOW: The ingredients of Cottage Garden Pot-pourri, shown here before drying. OPPOSITE: Six lovely, fragrant pot-pourris. Top to bottom: Autumn Spice (pine cones, leaves, cedar wood shavings, spices, daisies and marigolds); Summer Sherbet (citrus leaves, wood shavings, dried orange and lemon, daisies); Tudor Rose (roses); Natural Forest (ferns, acorns, chillies, berries, orange slices); Peach Daisy (peach slices, daisies, wood shavings); Strawberry Cinnamon (cinnamon, white daisies, star anise, leaves, strawberries).

PRESSING FLOWERS

Pressing flowers is a simple method of preserving the colour, shape and natural beauty of the blooms from your garden. Little equipment is needed and the pressed flowers can be easily stored until required.

 Pressing flowers preserves them as two-dimensional pictures. The flowers can be grouped together to make beautiful wall hangings, or they can be added to cards, gift tags, bookmarks, book covers, and even candles and the lids of wooden boxes and other containers.

COLLECTING FLOWERS FOR PRESSING

Not all flowers are equally suitable for pressing and you will need to experiment to find the best. For example, the amount of moisture in a flower will affect the result: as a general rule, the more succulent a flower or leaf is the less likely it is to retain its colour. Blue, red, pink and yellow flowers usually retain their colour well, while many white and pale pastel colours will turn brown. Smaller flowers press better than larger ones, and be sure to choose unmarked and well-shaped flowers and leaves to achieve a good quality finish. Some of the best flowers for pressing are delphiniums, geraniums, hydrangeas, lavender, pansies, polyanthus, roses, violas, violets and zinnias. Always collect flowers early in the day after the dew has evaporated from the petals.

Larger flowers such as roses will look best when the petals, sepals and leaves are individually pressed; sprays of flowers should be trimmed down so that the petals do not overlap; and bulky flowers should be cut in half.

Using pressed flowers

Pressed flowers make lovely cards. Purchase blank cards from craft stores or make them from cardboard. Arrange pressed flowers on top of the card, using forceps to position them. When you have the desired effect, squeeze a tiny amount of glue onto the end of a toothpick, apply it to the card where the flowers are to be positioned and then place the flowers on top of the glue. When creating a detailed design, glue down a few flowers and let them dry before adding the next few. This way they will not move out of place.

Bookmarks, book covers and pictures can be made in the same way, and pressed flowers can also be used to decorate glassware and wooden boxes. A thin coat of clear varnish can be painted gently over the flowers to protect them and extend their life.

RIGHT: Pictures, candles and cards: these are just some of the many ways you can use pressed flowers. The flower press pictured on the right makes the process easier but is not essential.

PRESSING FLOWERS

The flowers can either be put into a flower press or placed between sheets of blotting or other absorbent paper and then inserted inside books. When positioning the flowers be careful to make sure the petals will not crease or fold over once weight is applied to the press. Once the flowers are positioned between the paper, you need to apply constant pressure so that all the moisture is extracted from the plant material. If you are not using a flower press, place a heavy weight such as one or more bricks on the books.

As the moisture is squeezed out of the flowers and plant materials the paper becomes moist and will need to be replaced. (This is where a flower press comes into its own as changing paper layers in a press is simple and can be accomplished quickly.) Always mark the paper between the flowers with the date of pressing, so that the progress of the flowers can easily be monitored.

The paper will need to be changed every day for the first five days of pressing time if the colour of the flowers is to be retained. Then the flowers should be left in the press for about two weeks. (The time will vary between two and six weeks, depending on the size of the flowers and how succulent they are.) Check the flowers every two weeks in case the paper needs to be changed.

Equipment

Very little special equipment is needed to press flowers. Although a flower press is useful for large quantities, it is not essential. Placing flowers between sheets of blotting paper in books weighted down with bricks is equally effective.

Forceps are used to pick up delicate material, pointed scissors to trim foliage and flowers, and toothpicks to apply glue to the back of the dried flowers and foliage. A rubber-based glue or one that does not dry hard will make it easy to manipulate the flowers into a design.

INDEX

Published by Merehurst Limited, 1999
Ferry House, 51-57 Lacy Road, Putney, London SW15 1PR

ISBN S460/1 85391-772-9

COMMISSIONING EDITOR: Helen Griffin
SERIES EDITOR: Graham Strong
TEXT: Graham Strong and Roger Mann
EDITORS: Valerie Duncan and Christine Eslick
ILLUSTRATOR: Matthew Ottley
DESIGNER: Bill Mason
PUBLISHER: Anne Wilson

Printed by Tien Wah Press

The extract from *Lark Rise to Candleford* by Flora Thompson is taken
from the 1993 edition published by Cresset Press and reproduced by
permission of Oxford University Press.

PHOTOGRAPHS:

All photographs by Lorna Rose except
Valerie Duncan: *pp65 bottom right*
Joe Filshie and Andre Martin: *pp1, 76–78, 80–91*
Denise Greig: *pp27 centre*
Stirling Macoboy: *pp28 bottom, 30 bottom*
Merehurst: *pp2 top left and right, 3, 5, 6, 7, 8 right, 52 centre, 53 top and bottom,
66 top left and right, 71*
Clive Nichols: *front cover, pp61 bottom right (Ashtree Cottage, Wiltshire/
Designer Wendy Lauderdale)*
Photos Horticultural: *pp34 bottom, 45 bottom, 50 top, 54 centre*
Tony Rodd: *pp26 top*
Graham Strong: *pp8 left, 9, 10, 11, 12, 13, 14, 15, 16, 17, 18, 19, 23 top and centre,
33 centre and bottom, 34 top and centre, 35 bottom, 37 top and middle, 41 centre, 42 top,
46 centre and bottom, 52 top, 62, 69, 72, 73, 74, 75, 79, back cover*

Front cover: Red poppies
Title page: Bring your cottage garden inside with a delicate cut flower
arrangement